This is My New Foundation

Bill Bailey

This is My New Foundation

Copyright © 2025 by William Bailey
All rights reserved.

No part of this publication may be reproduced in whole or in part, stored in a retrieval system, or transmitted in any form or by any means—electronic, mechanical, photocopying, recording, or otherwise—without the prior written permission of the publisher, except in the case of brief quotations used in critical articles and reviews.

Library of Congress Cataloging-in-Publication Data
This Is My New Foundation
Published by Rapier Publishing
ISBNs
EBook: 979-8-218-80112-0
Paperback: 979-8-218-80111-3
Hard Cover: 979-8-218-80070-3

Printed in the United States of America

First Edition, 2025

Legal Disclaimer for the Book

Disclaimer

The views, thoughts, and opinions expressed in this memoir are solely those of the author and do not reflect the official policy or position of Rapier Solutions, its clients, affiliates, or partners. This book is based on personal experiences and reflections, and is not intended to disclose confidential or proprietary information.

This Is My New Foundation

A Memoir of Loss, Faith, and Rebuilding from the Shadows of COVID-19-

— Based on a True Story —

"What broke me didn't bury me. It built something stronger."

You are not alone in the forest.

Praise for **This Is My New Foundation**

"This Is My New Foundation is more than a memoir—it's a blueprint for resilience. Bill Bailey takes readers on a raw, unfiltered journey through trauma, faith, and redemption with unshakable honesty. His story reminds us that even in the darkest chapters, hope still has a voice. Inspiring, unforgettable, and deeply human."

—Early Reader Review

"Bill Bailey's story is a testament to the human spirit. This Is My New Foundation reminds us that rock bottom can be the start of something holy. Every page is filled with honesty, grit, and grace."

—Advance Reader Review

"Bill Bailey's writing doesn't just tell a story—it invites you into it. With a voice that's both intimate and unflinching, he writes like he's speaking directly to your heart. Every page reads smooth and clear, yet carries the weight of a life truly lived."

—Advance Reader Review

Amazon Editorial Description (Style-Focused):

Written with clarity, heart, and striking honesty, *This Is My New Foundation* delivers more than a memoir—it offers a conversation between author and reader. Bill Bailey's straightforward style makes even the most complex emotions feel accessible. With short, engaging paragraphs and powerful reflections, this book is as easy to read as it is hard to forget. Perfect for fans of real-life redemption stories, spiritual resilience, and memoirs that read like one-on-one conversations.

This Is My New Foundation

A Memoir of Loss, Faith, and Redemption — Based on a True Story

What do you do when the world goes quiet—and all you can hear is your past?

In This Is My New Foundation, Bill Bailey—veteran, entrepreneur, and survivor—strips away the layers of a life built on resilience, forged in trauma, and transformed by truth. From Detroit's streets to war's frontlines, from childhood wounds to corporate boardrooms, Bailey offers an unflinching account of survival, loss, love, and the long journey to healing.

This memoir isn't about easy victories. It's about storms that strip everything bare—and the faith, family, and fierce determination required to rebuild. With raw honesty and profound insight, Bailey reveals the moments that shaped him: buried trauma, the uniform that gave purpose, the pandemic that brought him to his knees, and the quiet strength that emerged from rubble.

This is a journey of spiritual growth, of learning to walk again—not just physically, but spiritually. It's about how God's grace, forgiveness, and renewed purpose transform brokenness into foundation. Through therapy, prayer, and faith, Bailey reconstructed not just his life—but his soul.

This is My New Foundation

More than redemption, This Is My New Foundation is a call to courage—for anyone who's felt broken, silenced, or left behind. It declares that healing is possible, even after the deepest wounds. It proves that no matter how cracked your ground appears, you can build something unshakable.

This is more than a memoir. This is a testimony of God's grace.

Navigating the Storm: A Veteran-Owned Business That Endures

Rapier Solutions — Built to Endure, Driven to Serve

In This Is My New Foundation, I candidly share the challenges Rapier Solutions faced during some of the most uncertain times—particularly at the height of the COVID-19 pandemic. Like many small businesses, we were tested in ways we never could have anticipated. Yet, what mattered most was how we responded.

As a veteran-owned company forged in discipline, service, and resilience, Rapier Solutions did more than simply weather the storm—we adapted. Guided by faith, fueled by innovation, and anchored by an unwavering commitment to our mission, we refocused, retooled, and emerged stronger. The outcome of that difficult season was not a company weakened by hardship, but one refined by it.

Our mission remained steadfast: to deliver dependable, high-impact solutions to both our private and government partners. We transformed challenges into catalysts for growth, driven by a dedicated team and a profound sense of purpose.

Today, Rapier stands as a sound and resilient organization—built to endure, driven to serve, and prepared to meet the evolving needs of those we support. The story of Rapier is not one of defeat, but of transformation—and that spirit lies at the heart of this book.

Acknowledgments

To my wife, Hazel

Your love has been my anchor, my covering, and my constant. Through the highs, the storms, and the silence, you never gave up on me. You stood by me when I couldn't stand by myself. Your patience, your strength, and your quiet faith reminded me that I am never alone. This foundation—this healing—was only possible because you helped hold the pieces while I learned how to put them back together. I love you deeply and endlessly.

To my children

You are my heart. You are the legacy I will always be proud of. Watching you grow, rise, and live your own truths has given my life purpose beyond words. I haven't always gotten everything right, but I've always loved you with everything I had. You've taught me grace. You've taught me joy. And you've reminded me, over and over again, why the fight to become better was worth it. I cherish each of you.

To My Sister

I never realized until writing this book that I might not be here if it weren't for you. I was five, in the bathroom for some reason, choking on a fish bone—in silence. You didn't panic—you acted fast.

This is My New Foundation

You knew if I cried out, Mom wouldn't let me eat fish again. So you stayed calm, brave, and quiet.

Thank you for saving my life. I'll never forget it.

Dedication

This book is dedicated to my mother, **Catherine Browder** whose unwavering strength, silent sacrifices, and unconditional love gave me the foundation to stand and the courage to speak. I've always believed she was born in the wrong decade, a modern-day woman ahead of her time.

And to my brother, **Marion "Money" Browder**
my best friend, my mirror, my reminder that even in pain,
there can be purpose.
Your voice still echoes in my spirit,
and this book carries your light.

Disclaimer

This memoir is a true account based on the author's memories, experiences, and perspectives. While every effort has been made to ensure accuracy, certain names, locations, and identifying details may have been changed to protect the privacy of individuals.

The views and reflections expressed in this book are those of the author and do not necessarily represent the opinions of any organizations, institutions, or individuals mentioned. This book is not intended to provide legal, medical, or psychological advice.

Some content may be sensitive or triggering for readers. Reader discretion is advised.

Table of Contents

This Is My New Foundation 5

Author's Note 16

Prologue: The Child in the Shadow: A Life of Duty and Determination 18

Chapter 1: 22

The Roots Beneath the Stone Survival, Secrets, and the Making of a Man 22

Chapter 2: 51

Hardy; The Quiet Storm 51

Chapter 3: 61

My Military Career 61

Discipline, Disillusionment, and the Man I Became 61

Chapter 4: 72

From the Shadows of COVID-19 72

Chapter 5: 85

A Reunion to Remember Honoring the Past Before Everything Changed 85

Chapter 6: 93

A Beautiful Escape from the Weight of Memory 93

Chapter 7: 100

The Onset of the Storm 100

When the World Changed—and So Did I 100

Chapter 8: 107

The Battle of My Mind vs Reality Confronting the Invisible War Within 107

Chapter 9: 116

A Future Forged from Resilience Turning Setbacks into Strength and Pain into Purpose 116

Chapter 10: 121

The Blessing in the Storm 121

Chapter 11: 129

This Is My New Foundation A Life Rebuilt from the Ground Up 129

Chapter 12: 134

A Life Shaped by Truth Owning My Story, Honoring My Scars 134

Chapter 13: 139

There's One More Truth 139

Chapter 14: 145

Forged in Pain; What Tried to Break Me, Built Me 145

Chapter 15: 149

Strengthened by Love; The Quiet Force That Kept Me Standing 149

Chapter 16: 157

Reclaiming Life During COVID-19 on the River 157

Chapter 17: 163

Marion "Money" Browder – The Brother Who Taught Me Grace 163

Chapter 18: 169

A Son Who Loved His Mom with Respect—By Any Means 169

Chapter 19: 179

This Is My New Foundation 179

Epilogue: This Is My New Foundation 183

A Life Built on Truth, Forged in Pain, Strengthened by Love, and Guided by Faith 183

Final Chapter: To You, the Reader 189

Seasons of a Man 194

Lessons Learned — Introduction 199

Author Bio 239

Author's Note

I want to take a moment to acknowledge something personal. As someone who has lived with **dyslexia,** writing this book wasn't easy—but it was necessary. The words you're reading didn't come without struggle. There were moments when letters blurred, sentences flipped, and frustration crept in. But I kept going.

This book is not about perfection—it's about truth. And if you've ever been told you couldn't, shouldn't, or wouldn't because of how your mind works, let this be proof that your story still deserves to be told.

Dyslexia didn't stop me from writing a book. It reminded me that every word matters, especially when it's written from the heart.

If you see a typo, a missed mark, or an imperfect sentence—thank you for your grace. This is my new foundation, built not in spite of the struggle, but through it.

Parents who are reading this book, remember:

Dyslexia can present challenges in your child's life, but it is manageable with the right approach and support. Many individuals with dyslexia are exceptionally creative, strategic thinkers, and innovative problem-solvers. With proper support, encouragement, and the child recognizing their

This is My New Foundation

strengths, your child can not only succeed academically but also grow with confidence and resilience.

With gratitude,

Bill Bailey

Prologue: The Child in the Shadow: A Life of Duty and Determination

Some people are born into privilege, while others are raised in chaos. Then there are those of us who carve a life out of fire, forged by fire of pain and the echoes of survival. I'm one of those people.

My story is not linear; it's not a straightforward climb from struggle to success. It's jagged, filled with losses, triumphs, second chances, and hard truths. From growing up in a home where trauma was wrapped in silence to becoming a Warrant Officer in the U.S. Army and successful small business from scratch—I've lived a life that doesn't fit neatly into boxes.

My life has been defined by discipline, sacrifice, and the determination to create something better—first for myself, then for my family, and eventually for my community. I have worn many uniforms: son, soldier, entrepreneur, husband, father. In each role, I learned something about who I was and who I was becoming.

But nothing prepared me for the invisible war that would come with the COVID-19 pandemic.

When the world stopped, so did I. The pandemic that stole lives and livelihoods also forced me to confront truths I had buried for decades. I was always the one people leaned on—

stable, strong, and self-reliant. But in the stillness, I found myself facing questions I had long ignored.

Was I really, okay? Had I made the right decisions—for my company, my people, and my family? Had I truly faced the ghosts of my past, or had I simply outrun them, heart pounding, hoping they would never catch me?

During COVID-19, I made decisions rooted in loyalty and duty. I kept my employees on payroll using government-backed loans because I believed in protecting those who built my company. I followed public health guidelines because I wanted to be responsible. I trusted systems I believed were there to help.

But hindsight has its own kind of brutal honesty. The lockdowns, the mandates, the isolation—they all came at a cost. I watched my business buckle under policies that seemed detached from reality. I watched family's fracture, including my own. I watched myself unravel in the silence, thread by thread.

The weight of it all forced a deeper reckoning—not just with the present, but with the scars of the past. Memories I had boxed up long ago clawed their way back into the light. Pain, I thought I had buried roared back with a force I wasn't ready for. I saw patterns—not just in my choices, but in the survival mechanisms I had mistaken for identity.

For the first time in my life, I couldn't outwork it. I couldn't lead my way around it. I had to feel my way through the darkness.

This story isn't about blame. It's not about politics. It's not even about COVID-19—not really.

It's about what happens when the world stops, and you're left alone with your reflection. It's about what it means to rebuild—not just a business, but a man. It's about discovering that the hardest battles are fought in silence, and the fiercest victories are the ones no one else sees. This is the story of how I lost nearly everything—and how I found something stronger waiting for me on the other side: myself

Chapter 1:

The Roots Beneath the Stone
Survival, Secrets, and the Making of a Man

My life as a child was a survival course rather than an adventure—no gentle landings, no safety nets, and most definitely no charts. Life didn't happen slowly; it hit me hard, quickly, and unexpectedly. It seemed like someone tore up my life's screenplay every four or five years and delivered it to me with a new cast, a new stage, and a new set of rules I had to follow to survive. I grew up struggling to survive each day; I was not given the luxury of dreaming.

A child raised in the circumstances I did—instability, abandonment, emotional neglect, and recurrent displacement—faces profound, multifaceted, and lasting psychological and emotional effects. To keep secure, you become extremely watchful and interpret faces, emotions, and tones. Trust is difficult to learn, but once you do, it becomes a valuable asset to hold on to. You replace plans—plans to escape, to adapt, to survive—with dreams. Youngsters like me frequently become hypervigilant, always looking out for danger. Establishing secure attachments is challenging for us. We often lose our sense of self and repress our feelings to survive. However, resilience is something else that develops in the shadow of all that suffering.

Because survival necessitates it, we develop intuition, empathy, and strategic thinking.

When my mother met Marion Jones when I was three, everything began to change. Marion Jones was a remarkable and unforgettable individual. There was no mistaking his presence, and he stood tall. He had a beautiful, radiant complexion due to his light brown skin, and he was renowned for having "very good hair," a term that, in some cultures, refers to hair that is exceptionally soft, fine, or manageable and is frequently associated with pride and admiration. One of Marion's most recognizable characteristics was his single gold tooth, which gave his smile a striking, yet ostentatious, touch and conveyed a sense of flair and confidence. He stood out everywhere he went, thanks to his attractive appearance, as well as this quality.

Marion Jones had the personality and atmosphere of a man who had just walked out of a song or a narrative. His personality is aptly encapsulated by the allusion to Jim Croce's famous song, "Bad, Bad Leroy Brown," which tells the story of a tough, stylish, and dangerous man. Marion exuded toughness, confidence, and maybe a touch of danger, just like Leroy Brown. Not only was he attractive, but he had a charismatic aura that would last with you long after you met him.

To put it briefly, Marion Jones was a man with streetwise charm and the kind of personality that lived up to the tale of a song. He was also smooth, stylish, and captivating.

My upbringing was no longer mine once Marion Jones met my mother.

Marion Jones was the object of my mother's intense devotion, which ultimately led to my demise. Marion had a captivating appearance that drew people's attention.

My reality changed more times between the ages of six and ten than many individuals experience in their lives. There were never two years that were alike. Some houses had the feel like traps, while others were pit stops. Like a note nobody wanted to read, I was passed from hand to hand. Officially, these weren't foster homes. They were my mother's friends and family. I didn't realize at the time that being a light-skinned boy made me desirable. As my mother pursued her dream with Marion, others wanted to adopt me, take me in, or just let me stay.

I always got along well with Marion. However, I reminded my mother of a man who wasn't him. I wasn't his son. I, therefore, realized I didn't fit in with her new way of living, even if he never yelled at me. My other siblings were twelve (Hardy), ten (Rita), and eight (Larry) years older than I, so I don't remember them living with us. They have started their own lives, and I was the one left behind, feeling like the oldest child of my brother, Money, and my sister, Nicole.

You only know the world that is shown to you when you are a youngster. You view neglect as merely another form of quiet and instability, as usual. Since then, I've seen women who would never pick a man over their child, but I don't blame my mom. She had fallen in love. Furthermore, when love is at its most intense and blinding, it can cause people to lose sight of who they are or the people they are meant to protect.

Amid all that craziness, I discovered how to live. I was forced to. Before COVID, I was able to repress painful experiences in my life by using my imagination. The nightmares then came to life.

My mother never completely accepted me as a child. There was an invisible wall between us that I could not get over, no matter how hard I tried. I could feel it, but I could not find the right words to say it. As I got older, I learned the truth: I was not my stepfather's son. That unstated truth appeared to define our relationship and put a wall between us that I could not get over. I knew I did not fit into the new life she had made, but I stayed with her, hoping that things might change one day.

I mostly spent my days with Butchie and Auntie Minnie before I reached nine. Butchie lived above a local pub and was a strong, no-nonsense woman. 8231 12th W Side N Seward SW Detroit,

This is My New Foundation

Michigan, is home to the Chit Chat Lounge. Throbbed beneath us, a musical heartbeat in Detroit. It attracted icons like Motown's house band and the Funk Brothers and was more of a refuge than a bar. That stage was dominated by the legendary keyboardist Earl Van Dyke. My earliest recollections were framed by the sounds and smells of fried food, spilled liquor, and music that permeated the floorboards like incense. Music didn't just play there—it lingered, like incense in a church. Somehow, by grace or destiny, I crossed paths with Robert Kennedy, Dr. Martin Luther King Jr., and Muhammad Ali—all before the age of ten. My life was rooted in the rhythm of Detroit.

Cigarette smoke swirled, jukebox soul flowed through her apartment over the bar, and the unvarnished laughter of ladies who had seen too much life to sugarcoat anything reverberated. Butchie, a white woman who never tried to hide who she was, lived there with me.

As a lesbian, she was straightforward, unrepentant, and strong. During the day, her world revolved around Ford, and at night, she would go to Chit Chat Loung, which I usually call the bar. While she was taking a bath, I would sit on the toilet lid and observe her through the steam, not knowing what I was seeing. To me, she was a mystery—a power that was both unpredictable and protective. I was aware even then that I was in an area that straddled the boundary between safety and peril.

One Saturday evening, the threat revealed itself.

As usual, Butchie had gone to the bar downstairs. The sound of the bass hammering through the floorboards soothed me while I slept upstairs. After that, something changed. She was asked to dance by a man. "No," she said. He slapped her. She slashed his arm with a knife. It ought to have ended there. However, he returned with a vengeance two hours later. She died immediately beneath the flat after he shot her in the bar.

Although I didn't hear the shooting, I do recall the yelling, the ensuing confusion, the frantic footsteps on the stairs, and the people calling my name. Silent and motionless, I snuggled myself beneath the cover in the hopes that the horror would pass me by if I remained motionless.

I came to the icy reality that the world doesn't give a damn about your age or innocence after that night. Even so, trauma can find you.

My surroundings weren't simply unsteady when I was seven years old; they were boiling. Standing on street corners where revolution buzzed in the air like electricity, I peddled publications for the Black Panthers. I sensed the power and the sense of purpose, even though I didn't completely get the politics. Occasionally, my aunt would come to visit or take me for a weekend, and then she would draw me close and murmur that I was "special." I didn't feel unique at the time; therefore, I didn't see it. I experienced a sense of displacement. Perhaps she recognized a spark in me that I was unaware I possessed, a seed that would not perish in any kind of soil.

By 1969, Israel and Egypt were engaged in a low-level but lethal war along the Suez Canal. It was an unrelenting slog of commando raids, airstrikes, and artillery engagements known as the War of Attrition. The area teetered on the verge of full-scale conflict as Egypt, supported by the Soviet Union, became more belligerent every day.

I wrote to President Nixon—yes, that Nixon—about the situation of the Jews, somehow, in the middle of all that far-off strife and uncertainty. I was assisted in addressing it to the White House by one of my teachers. I was unable to pinpoint the precise reason for my writing urge. The question was rooted in something more profound than comprehension. I just felt the weight of it. Something about that struggle resonated with me, even as a child, amid my upheaval.

Then—he replied in writing.

An actual letter. An authentic signature.

It seemed to a boy from shattered homes and fractured sidewalks that someone in the sky had spoken, "I see you." The letter sparked something inside of me, but it didn't completely alter my reality. It served as a reminder that I was important despite the chaos and neglect.

The violence increased in 1969, the same year. My father's sister, my aunt Maude, was killed in a drug house. She resided in a building on Windermere and Blaine in Detroit, down the hall from Marion Jones, my mother, my brother Money, and me. The Nation of Islam was meant to keep that neighborhood safe. No drugs. No merchants. Not a problem.

Evil, however, disregards laws and limits and acts by its desires.

According to the authorities, everyone inside had been fatally stabbed and bound. It was more than simply a murder; it was a cruel warning to the dealers to stay away. Even if I didn't fully comprehend it at the time, I could feel its effects. My experience with death was not the first, nor will it be the last. Death was thus more than a shadow; it was a housemate.

Despite everything, I managed to find faith.

It grew silently inside of me, but I can't recall when it started. In my sleep, God appeared to me in dreams—visions even—as calm, substantial, and present. I requested to get baptized when I was ten years old. I knew I needed something pure to cling to—something that couldn't be taken, corrupted, or destroyed—but no one told me to.

I sensed God's presence even in the dark as if He were hovering just over the brink, supporting me when everything else threatened to topple me.

In July 1967, Detroit was consumed by one of the most intense and devastating civil disturbances in U.S. history — the 12th Street Riot. At the time, I was just a child, living right in the middle of the chaos, on 12th Street and Blaine. I didn't hear about the riot on the television. Instead, it was the sounds of sirens, the sharp crack of gunfire, and the acrid smoke that filled the air outside our window. Even though I didn't understand the politics or racial tensions that led to the violence, I could feel the fear and anxiety that gripped our neighborhood. It was the kind of mayhem you never forget. I was there in the middle of three riots in Detroit. I was living history, not merely witnessing it.

At that moment, I spotted Miss Brickton, my first-grade teacher, whom I will always remember. Despite the turmoil around us, she walked through the neighborhood with quiet authority. She was a white woman, overweight and pleasant but severe. She guided every Black child home as if it were her sacred duty, remaining composed while others panicked. Every child we passed would pause and say, "Hello, Miss Brickton," as we moved in a single file. She would reply in her trademark fashion without missing a beat: "You are wrong for burning down the neighborhood." Those six words were her hallmark, regardless of what else had been spoken. Those kids didn't challenge it. They held her in high regard. The majority of children had learned from her in our early years, and she was still teaching at that precise moment, leading with presence rather than fear. I lived through the riots in Detroit, not just reading about them in a textbook. It happened three times. The sound of broken glass, smoke, and sirens wasn't background noise. That was the cadence of my early years.

I sensed the tension—the way the air became heavy, as if the city were holding its breath—even though the adults didn't say much. I recall my mother yanking us back from the window as if it were attempting to draw us in, our faces illuminated by the orange glow of the fire and the scent of rubber and anger.

This is My New Foundation

At noon, the smoke darkened the sky. Overhead, helicopters hovered like irate insects. On the streets where we used to ride our bikes, tanks rolled. I witnessed neighbors bringing food out of broken grocery store windows to feed families who had gone hungry long before the glass broke, not to steal.

We were referred to as looters. Thugs. Creatures. However, nobody ever inquired as to why the city blew up. The fact that survival has always been a silent riot for us was ignored.

I was living history at the time, but I was unaware of it amidst all the chaos. And I don't have to search for information when people ask me where I was during the riots in Detroit decades later.

I was present.

Following the assassination of Dr. Martin Luther King Jr. in 1968, the sadness in our community evolved into something more intense and depressing. Once more, the streets were crowded. The city was burning from the inside out when I peered out the window. This was sorrow, not simply a rage.

But despite all of that suffering, an odd thing occurred. The Detroit Tigers advanced to the World Series the same year. In 1968, the World Series was the pinnacle of American sports— bigger than the Super Bowl, more celebrated, and deeply woven into the national identity. I recall the huge, cumbersome box

This is My New Foundation

TVs on carts that the schools used to carry into every classroom. As the Tigers defeated the St. Louis Cardinals, we all sat there, cheering together, our eyes wide. The city felt like one team for a while. We all wanted to win, regardless of age or color.

Kids usually just go about their lives, but I? I experienced history. I felt it molding me, minute by minute, rather than merely seeing it happen. Detroit taught me the world, even though my brother Hardy taught me the streets.

I wasn't truly a child by the time I reached my twelfth birthday. I had done things no youngster should have done and seen things I shouldn't have seen. My older sister's pals and some of my mother's friends would invite me to stay the night. Until you find out what "spending the night" implies, that seems harmless.

I would eventually find myself in an adult woman's bed.

Those nights were devoid of tenderness. No affection. Only possession. I was a body, an object, a presence that gave them a sense of power or well-being or whatever perverse desire they were attempting to satiate. I wasn't even sure I could talk about it, let alone know how. By doing things around the house and providing these women with a "man's presence," my mother most likely believed that I was being helpful. However, I was a child playing a part that no child should ever have to play; I wasn't a man.

The women who visited our home appeared to be cordial enough; some were family friends, others were distant relatives, and most were my sister's friends, who were often ten years my senior.

They were always smiling—syrupy, practiced smiles—offering compliments that floated like smoke and gifts so small they barely existed. By the time I was ten, I'd seen more naked women than most people had drunk cans of Coke. I had become oddly skilled at giving massages, my hands moving with a familiarity that no child should possess—most often while they lay stretched out in nothing but their bra and panties.

Their actions occasionally appeared strange, a little out of balance, but a child's eyes were blind to the underlying currents of manipulative behavior. These days, hearing the name Dennis brings back memories of those women, even if you are not related. In the 1960s and early 1970s, the majority of the ladies wore wigs. I feel the need to avoid women who wear wigs as I've become older.

I would gladly accept their praise and threats without questioning the ulterior motives underlying their innocuous behavior. Their touch, which occasionally lingered longer than necessary, was dismissed as simple affection and a typical aspect of adult communication. However, there was a subtle change in their behavior around me, an unspoken, intimate language that

I was still learning to understand. It wasn't until I reached adulthood that I realized what predatory conduct meant. I considered a grown woman putting her hands down my trousers to be normal.

Maslow's Theory of Human Motivation states that when someone's basic safety requirements are consistently unmet, such as when predatory behavior is misperceived as harmless, as in the case of "spending the night," hypervigilance may result. The typical course of psychological development is disturbed by this kind of behavior, in which persons in positions of authority push a youngster into adult settings. The person remains obsessed with protection and survival rather than moving toward higher-level desires, such as love, esteem, and self-actualization. In reaction to persistent trauma and exploitation, hypervigilance turns into a coping strategy—constant alertness. This protective mood demonstrates how abuse warps the normal course of human motivation and emotional development and represents an unfulfilled need for protection as defined by Maslow's hierarchy.

I became who I am because of this.

I had been working for years by the time I was twelve, doing odd jobs, hustles, anything to gain some extra cash or learn something new. I was naturally good with electronics. I couldn't resist disassembling anything with wires, such as radios and TVs, to see how they operated.

My curiosity finally overcame me one day, and I opened our TV, stereo, and record player. I had to find out how that man entered the tube. As I disassembled it, I labeled each wire, screw, and tube, arranging them exactly as I had seen in repair guides in my mind. Having dyslexia has given me a unique ability to recognize and remember patterns. But that day finished with a whipping because I didn't have enough time before my folks returned home.

I remember that moment because it was the first time someone looked at me with purpose, not merely because I didn't completely understand the danger. One of my numerous odd tasks as a child was assigned by Mr. Hill, the local TV repairman. However, he noticed something happening rather than a restless youngster obstructing the path or creating a mess. He felt called. He saw that God was already working in me, molding me into something greater than I could have ever dreamed.

Another memory emerges when I work through my trauma and go back to those pivotal times; it starts as a whisper from the past. The year is 1986. In the Army, I work as a mainframe repairman out of a mobile van with my computer repair crew. A loose ground wire was causing an unstable connection, which was the result of a malfunctioning transformer.

This is My New Foundation

I had to manually reset it every morning, moving the bulky transformer back into position to restore electricity. It was now standard procedure. Muscle memory. Nothing noteworthy. Until my hand dropped one morning.

A black line burned through the metal like paper when 600 volts suddenly arced through the screwdriver I was holding. The sound, the brightness, and the heat all occurred more quickly than anticipated. However, it left a mark on more than just the instrument. I was at fault. A reminder that we live on the brink. The distinction between obligation and hazard is extremely hazy.

It wasn't until I noticed the scorch mark that I realized what had happened. There was a moon brunt in the center of the 1" screwdriver. After glancing at me, my platoon sergeant, SFC Turner, said, "You're no good to me today." Return home and recuperate.

As soon as I arrived home, I could still clearly hear Mr. Hill's voice saying, "That'll happen if you're not careful," as if he were standing next to me once more.

However, I realized then that it was grace, not caution. I might have suffered severe injuries. I might have disappeared. However, I wasn't.

God was still in control of me, as He always was. The teachings are never-ending. Life offers us lessons every day, but we must pay attention. The warnings can occasionally be sent by individuals such as those suffering or experiencing near misses, but they are always heavenly messages.

And if you're smart, you learn to develop from the lessons rather than just get by.

Before turning 10, I also worked at the local fruit and vegetable market, where I cleaned greens and snapped the ends off green beans, and I sold newspapers. For $1, I even picked up trash at the nearby church. I felt wanted and useful at work as if I had some influence over at least one aspect of my day.

And sometimes, a child just needs a reason to feel important.

I had never really dealt with technology or business before. A spark in the storm's midst. A steady thing was growing inside of me while everything else in my world seemed to be collapsing. I was developing, learning, and honing a skill. And I was creating myself without even recognizing it. However, the burden of the previous actions never went away. The females. The evenings. The unsaid guilt. I was too familiar with my sister's friends. Their touch seemed intrusive rather than warm. They viewed me as a resource to be utilized as if I owed them something. I felt claimed—like property handed between hands—rather than loved. Lost innocence is a common topic of conversation. It was taken, but I kept mine. But I survived.

I discovered how to keep my head down, my soul up, and my faith intact while breathing through the pain. Because I remained upright despite the world's constant attempts to shatter me.

I had no mentor, no blueprint, and no roadmap to help me improve or get back on track. But no matter how bleak things got, I had resolve—a quiet, deep fire that would not go out. I used that fire as a compass. It kept me going even though it didn't make the journey simple or the suffering go away. On certain days, I ventured into the unknown, unsure of whether my next step would uplift or depress me.

I woke up in the middle of the night to the sound of my heart pounding like a warning bell—still here, still fighting. I used to converse with God during those times, especially when I was a kid, in the kind of low-key, frantic chatter that only a seven-year-old could have, not with pretentious prayers. I heard Him for the first time then, not in words but in a knowing. He assured me that I would be alright and that this was merely a phase I needed to experience. I somehow trusted Him even back then.

I choose to survive somewhere between the ache of being invisible and the pressure to be tough, between childhood trauma and adult responsibilities. And I lived. I didn't just barely—I persevered.

I would go on to lead a prosperous life a few decades later. I led teams without their knowing that I had once fixed TVs for food at the age of 10, and I signed contracts that opened doors. I had a lovely house with soft-close cupboards and granite worktops. I used to drive the fancy cars I saw in glass showroom windows. I visited places I never thought I'd see, including Rome, Havana, Iceland, and the Star Wars Yoda cave in Iceland. As a child, I sheltered under the covers while the outside world raged, and I ate in fancy restaurants and slept in rooms I could never have imagined.

To be clear, though, money did not erase the memories. My mental vaults of pain remained unemptied. The ghosts were not quieted by it. They had more space to move around—in still times, in quiet settings, in places that success cannot access. I had access to money but not to healing. It provided solace but no resolution. What I had endured was not undone by it. The young child inside me, who still yearned for safety, was not hugged by it. The deeper wounds remained, not as severe as before but persistent, like flickering shadows just outside the light. "Have you dealt with it yet?" they asked me in whispers all the time. The answer was no for a while. But I continued. Because when all else failed, resolve carried me. Because it had become instinctive to survive. And because I secretly thought that one day, I would rebuild rather than endure. This time, it came from trust, honesty, and a strength that no amount of money or phony buddy could match.

"All of humanity's problems stem from man's inability to sit quietly in a room alone" is a saying that I always carry with me, and that captures all I've experienced. Blaise Pascal was correct when he said that. I needed to learn how to sit in that room, not just quietly, but honestly. And that was the main thing that completed me.

The trauma never really went away. It was never gone, but it dwelt in the recesses of my memory like dust in a locked attic. As if my body remembered what my mouth had been unable to express for years, it occasionally came to the surface in nightmares, occasionally in the space between talks, and occasionally in the way I flinched when someone stood too close.

I served in the Army for 26 years, 13 of which were on active duty and 13 in the reserves. I recognized the familiarity of discipline where others did not. I had been trained by chaos long before the military. I was already a soldier in spirit when I put on my boots and saluted the flag. The Army gave that spirit to the organization. It gave me status, meaning, and a fraternity I believed would never waver. Even brotherhood, though, has its shadows.

One evening in 1982, I was stationed in Hawaii. I had picked up a girl with a friend. In the cadence of barracks culture, what began as just another evening swiftly changed. He refused to let her go when she expressed her desire to do so. Under a moonless sky, he took us far away from the streetlights and into a pineapple field. Something dark changed in his gaze, and I noticed it. I understood his intention. I refused, standing between them. I ruined everything, he added, calling me a fool. Perhaps I did. I ruined the right thing, though. Because I couldn't allow it to occur—not while I was around. Not after what I'd witnessed ladies go through. Not after what I had gone through. For me, that night redefined manhood, not just the termination of a friendship. Losing people is a part of being a man, but you never lose your soul.

The majority of my friendships seemed to terminate after four or five years. You pack up, start over, form new relationships, and produce a new body of work every few years, much like military duty rotations. Betrayal, pride, responsibility, and distance all take their toll. However, some friendships went further. Some roots remained. I still carry with me the ones that made it through service, divorce, sadness, and the awful silence of time.

I eventually created a life. I left the military. I started a firm from scratch and built it into a small, profitable enterprise. I became a grandfather after becoming a father. After three marriages that left me more damaged than better, I even discovered love again. However, something inside of me also shut down when the world went down in 2020. The silence broke my heart. Suddenly, the movement that had always held my past at bay ceased, and the memories flooded back. The past kicked in the darn door rather than knocking.

The kind of family get-together that we had all learned to cherish in uncertain times took place one calm night during the pandemic. The room was filled with casual talk and laughter around the card table, and for a while, everything seemed normal—until it didn't. A sister-in-law said something casual, not malicious or unkind, simply one of those unguarded things people say when they feel comfortable. She claimed that having sex with several men in one day made her feel alive. She was unaware of the feelings her comments evoked in me. Her words and presence sparked something that had been long buried. Unexpectedly, A face I hadn't thought of in years resurfaced without warning, and with it, the memory of one of the women who had taken advantage of me when I was just a child. What had been shut away suddenly returned, fresh and unwanted.

The problem with trauma is that it gets faster when you slow it down. It catches you. It will not be disregarded. It demands to be noticed. The women who should have protected me but instead treated me like property rushed back, the faces I thought I had outrun. The anguish did not return as anger or even sadness. It returned as knowledge, clarity, and a truth I could at last identify.

Nevertheless, there was happiness despite all of that suffering. My grandchildren are writing a new chapter, one that is lighter and more liberated than mine. My name is with them, but my trauma is not. And that's grace to me. To hold my children and laugh with them, I would drive for twelve hours straight, traveling across Canada from West Point to Detroit late on Friday nights. On Sunday, I would resume my duties as if nothing had happened. Love like that doesn't yell or call for applause. It simply arrives weary, remains there, and departs in silence. However, it is important. It's a living heritage.

I would say this to the younger me—the man who carried the burden of quiet, the youngster who hid under blankets—you don't simply grow up; you develop into the person you were destined to be. Even in the most difficult circumstances—through mistreatment, treachery, and loss—something lovely can blossom. Life may not be a flawless garden.

That is the start of my story.

Certain wounds mutter rather than shout. They inhabit the calm times, the voids between denial and recollection. Blame is not the topic of this chapter. The truth is at issue. The bravery to go back and recapture the power, rather than endure the agony, is what matters.

This is My New Foundation

Let me be clear from the bottom of my heart: I do not hate anyone. I have no resentment. I hope that everyone I have come into contact with finds serenity. May we all have the fortitude to defend what counts and the grace to recover.

I am not just telling this story to defend the child who I used to be. Every child deserves to feel protected, seen, and precious, and I am on watch for them. Because when silence ends, healing starts.

For the majority of my life, I was a people pleaser. Being one who never caused trouble, saying the right thing, and laughing at the right time were all skills I learned early on to make people feel at ease. It was not a talent. It was a matter of survival.

When I reached adolescence, that calm, amiable disposition put me in a predicament I did not completely comprehend.

In the past, we shared a four-family apartment building in Detroit with Mike and Angie, a young couple, on Hartwell Street. Mike had a job in the automobile sector. Angie was a homemaker. They appeared to be a picture-perfect couple from the outside. They took my brother and me to church services, movies, and local events. Perhaps nine or ten years older than us, they were generous and compassionate.

However, Mike would depart for his job. Additionally, Angie would summon me downstairs.

At the time, I was unsure of how to interpret it. I was able to keep a secret, though. She'd ask me to undress, lie on the couch behind her, and just hold her—no words, nothing to explain. Not a sound. It was just my body against hers. Not in a lighthearted manner. Not in a way that seemed appropriate. Simply... silence. On most days, she would doze off in that manner. I would, too, sometimes.

It wasn't aggressive. It wasn't loud. And that's precisely why it was so hard to understand. At twelve or thirteen, I didn't have the language to describe what was happening. It didn't register as abuse. It didn't fit the shape of what I thought harm looked like.

I only knew enough to feel that I shouldn't speak of it — that I should be embarrassed. And yet, in my young mind, I thought I was blessed. I believed I was claiming something of my body, of my place beside a woman. At that age, for a boy, that felt rare. Even special.

I also buried it. Deep.

That stillness became part of my daily habit for six months. I also played a role. The good boy. The assistant. The keeper of secrets. I did not tell my brother. I did not tell my mom. I never told myself the whole truth.

However, trauma never goes away. It does nothing but wait.

I was driving alone decades later, in the long, lonely silence of COVID-19, when the memory came back to me like a voice-riding shotgun. Angie was there all of a sudden, even though I had not thought about her in years. At last, it became evident to me that what she had done was unacceptable.

I was not at fault for how I felt.

There was no anger in that knowledge. It was clear. A firm conviction also accompanied it: I would never permit a child to carry the same level of silence that I did.

I don't let my grandchildren sit on my lap. Not even my children. Unlike other fathers or grandfathers, I never let them lean against me. It's not for lack of love—it's because of it. For years, I couldn't explain why. But the night my sister-in-law made that comment, something clicked. In that moment, I finally understood the root of my overprotectiveness, the reason I've always kept a careful distance from children: not to shield them from the world, but to shield them from something in me.

Because I can still recall the sensation of being caressed in a way that made it difficult to distinguish between perplexity and compassion. Because I am aware that what appears gentle, quiet, and even friendly can conceal harm.

I have drawn lines out of reverence rather than fear. To maintain innocence, not to keep a distance.

I wish I could hold them for longer sometimes. There are moments when I long for the intimacy I observe in other families. However, I have come to realize that tenderness is not always a sign of love. It appears to be a border at times. The kind of love that declares, "This will not happen under my watch," might occasionally be the strongest.

I, therefore, adore them in different ways. By being there. By giggling. By use of faith. They never have to wonder, thanks to safety.

My purpose in sharing this story is to speak, not to embarrass or accuse, because shame thrives in silence. What about my voice? I now own it.

In all honesty, though, I do not despise Angie. I do not harbor resentment. I would be happy to hear that she is doing well if I were to see her today. She was, in my opinion, a decent woman who endured her suffering. However, what transpired was important. And to defend others, I had to face it.

I lost something with Angie.

And I think that's when I began to understand: love and passion aren't the same as sex. Sometimes, what people truly need is love — warmth, connection, to be seen and held — and it can be mistaken for desire. For sex.

48

But they're not the same. And back then, I didn't know the difference.

She did not take away my power to defend, though.

That power—I took it back.

"Speak up for those who cannot speak for themselves; ensure justice for those being crushed."

Proverbs 31:8 (NLT)

Dedication

To the child I was, who carried uncertainty with a graceful silence.

To the man I have grown into, who opted for honesty over silence.

What began with a voice in the dark would echo through every decision I made. But first, I had to survive the silence of my childhood.

This is My New Foundation

CHAPTER 2
– HARDY – THE QUIET STORM
BASED ON 12TH STREET, DETROIT IN 60s AND 70s

*"The righteous man walks in his integrity;
his children are blessed after him."*
— Proverbs 20:7

Chapter 2:

Hardy; The Quiet Storm

There is always someone in every family who straddles the line between hero and outlaw. That was my brother Hardy on my mind. You've probably seen someone like him on The Wire—fearless, streetwise, and full of paradoxes. Omar was close, but Hardy's presence was even more potent. With just silence, he could dominate a room. He didn't have to say much because his stance, eyes, and whole demeanor spoke for him. Before he even spoke, everyone sensed him, so they paid attention.

Not only was he respected, but he was respected cautiously. With strong shoulders from years of boxing and street life, long curly hair that cascaded down his back, and a style that made his red Mustang seem like an extension of himself, Hardy was a handsome and hard-edged man. Heads turned as Hardy rolled through the neighborhood. People either stepped aside or smiled.

Hardy was tough on the outside, but he was gentle inside, especially to me and my brother Money. He purchased all of our presents and created a magical atmosphere, ensuring that we had a truly wonderful Christmas that year. In a society that frequently ignored boys like me, the chemical set and "The Man from U.N.C.L.E. Attaché Case" were gifts that gave me a sense of significance.

However, I lost that Christmas before New Year's. Unaware of the hazard, I prepared sulfuric acid, a chemical compound, by myself in the flat. The apartment had to be evacuated because the fumes were so intense that nobody could breathe. The presents have vanished. That day, the spirit of Christmas vanished with the air. Hardy didn't reprimand or yell even then. His quiet seemed controlled rather than vicious, as though he was aware that I was already receiving a harsh lesson. Hardy never touched me.

All he said to me was, "You are intelligent. Continue attending classes. Avoid skipping. Nothing is available for you out in these streets. "Don't be like me" was the most significant lesson he ever taught me.

I recall putting paper in the toes of Hardy's shoes because they were too large for me to wear. Because I was wearing Hardy's shoes to school. Even though my feet didn't quite fit his shoes, I only wanted to feel a little closer to him —to act and look like him, to follow in his footsteps. I prepared for the storm when he learned. But rather than blowing up, he just remarked, "Dennis, have you been wearing my shoes?" while glancing at me.

I remembered that moment.

This is My New Foundation

You'll see the several names I've gone by throughout my life as you continue reading. I was Dennis at home. My name was William at school. Then, in 1988, I was referred to as Bill Bailey by a female lecturer who was also a West Point major. She adored the way it came naturally to her, and soon, everyone else did the same. Thus, keep this in mind when you read these pages: The boys, Dennis and William, are both younger than eighteen. The man I have become is Bill.

Let's go back to the shoes.

I informed him, "Yeah, but I fixed them all." He verified that each pair had brand-new soles and heels, which I had fixed with the cash I had saved from delivering papers and mowing lawns. His eyes were steady as he returned. "Stay out of my shoes," he commanded.

That was it. Don't yell. Not a threat. Only Hardy.

Our Uncle John once pulled me aside and said, "Dennis, you and Hardy are going to have it out one day. And when it happens, use anything you can to protect yourself—because Hardy can fight, and if he can't beat you with his hands, there's no telling what he's capable of." He said it like a certainty, not a possibility. Like a fuse already lit, just waiting to reach the powder.

However, that day never materialized.

Despite Hardy's fury and edge, our confrontation never took place. Perhaps it was a matter of respect. Perhaps it was self-control. Perhaps there was more to it. In any case, the battle Uncle John forewarned me about remained in the realm of hypothetical scenarios.

I now think that, much as I aspired to be like Hardy as a kid, a part of him was also observing me—observing what is made possible when potential and opportunity collide. I believe he recognized that in me. I was winning everything at school, at least until the eighth grade. In the Christmas play, I was the main character. All of the math and science prizes went to me. I gave them hope that an opportunity was achievable in a family when opportunities were limited, as if one of us might succeed.

Hardy didn't have to speak louder. His quiet was a powerful statement.

Two of my friends and I believed we would become criminals in 1973. With the help of James Brown's anthem, The Boss, and the film Black Caesar, we had it all laid out in our impressionable brains. We got together with the man across the Street and devised a scheme to steal and sell clothing from Montgomery Ward, inspired and misled by him.

We each parked close to a different exit as we rode our bikes to the store. The plan was straightforward: one of us would enter the store with the others, grab as many shirts as we could, run out a side entrance, and ride away. Both runs went without a hitch. Without any problems, my friends managed to pull it off. But God had other ideas when it was eventually my turn. They caught me.

We were stealing shirts worth over $30 and selling them for around $10 each. When you were caught stealing in 1973, your parents were called instead of the cops. However, Hardy's silence was what affected me, not the cash or even the humiliation.

I was quickly disciplined after I was caught. I was whipped by my brother Larry. At my cousin's place, my sister Rita then beat me up once more. The longest bike ride of my life followed, and every pedal felt like a form of punishment. My mother also gave me a whipping when I eventually made it home. Hardy, however, waited.

"Where'd you get the idea to do something like that?" he questioned me calmly later that night when the storm had passed. I told the truth. I explained to him how the man across the Street had pledged to pay for whatever we were able to steal. Hardy simply responded, "I knew you were slick," and nodded. That was all.

That dude stopped talking to me the very following day. He never sat on his porch again. Hardy had dealt with it quietly, forcefully, and physically. He did it that way.

I was transformed by that moment. I never stole anything before, and that was the last time. At that point, I understood that attempting to be a gangster had a cost, and I wasn't prepared to pay it.

Being raised under Hardy's influence meant that we learned lessons about the world and our family at a young age. Additionally, it seemed as though the entire globe was on fire in Detroit during the 1960s and early 1970s.

I wanted to play ball everywhere in the city, whether it was on the east or west side, when I was seventeen. Hardy stopped me.

He declared, "You are not permitted on the east side."

I answered, "I haven't done anything to anyone."

He remarked, "You have." "You are my brother. That is sufficient.

He gave me a direct glance. "I'll beat you like a man if I catch you on the east side." Dennis, can you hear me?

I heard him.

Hardy knew the street politics—the names, the resentments, the blood debts—but he was not afraid of anyone. And he shielded me from all of them.

Hardy was the one who said goodbye to me when I enlisted in the Army in 1981. We ate dinner. Keep quiet. Actual. We did it that way.

It took me four years to go back home. Nobody knew Hardy's specific location when I did. However, he was waiting on my mother's porch the following day.

He remarked, "I saw you driving down Jefferson." "You look like no one else in the world."

We sat and conversed. It was the first time my daughters saw him. He treated them with the same gentleness that he had always shown me. We got back in touch.

He then told me about his time in prison and how he was apprehended in possession of stolen mink jackets. He heard kids sobbing in a different room while he waited for the fence. He phoned the cops since something didn't feel right. They located the coats and the children. He was taken into custody.

"Hardy, why did you call from your room?" said a police officer who knew him. We must now take you in.

"I should've handled those men myself," Hardy later told me. I wouldn't have served time then.

In 1988, when I returned home again, we met, and I had my military records with me. I let Hardy read my military 201 files, which included all my evaluations. "Those white folks like you," he added, turning to face me after he was done. It was pride, not judgment. "Assure me you will remain in the Army," he continued.

He was attacked by three males in a single altercation two weeks later. It was a hit; it wasn't arbitrary. "He would have killed us all tomorrow if we hadn't tried to kill him that day," one of the attackers subsequently told a judge. His adversaries were aware of his identity.

Hardy had requested a handgun I had from me while I was in Detroit that month. Silently. Not a drama. He didn't get it from me. I continued to try to live "right" while in uniform. I carried that decision like a stone in my chest after he was killed. What if I had handed that pistol to him? Would he still be here? I will never know. There is no answer to the question.

Hardy was more than just a brother—he was my mirror, my counselor, and my protector. He lived by a code, though he wasn't without flaws. When he urged me to stay in the Army, he wasn't asking me to follow in his footsteps. He was telling me to build my own path. Yes, I did.

Due to Hardy.

If there was light in those early years, it was often hidden behind shadows. The war inside my home soon taught me what war outside would look like.

CHAPTER 3
My Military Career
Discipline, Disillusionment, and the Man I Became

Chapter 3:

My Military Career
Discipline, Disillusionment, and the Man I Became

At the age of 20, I chose the red clay of Fort Sill, Oklahoma, over the rough edges of Detroit's streets. My Army journey started there. Ten weeks of Basic Combat Training and five weeks and four days of Advanced Individual Training at Fort Sill were necessary for Cannon Crewmember training. This time was divided between classroom instruction and fieldwork conducted in combat simulation settings. When I joined the Army, I stepped into something far beyond my understanding, a world that would challenge and shape me in ways I could never have anticipated. It offered direction, stability, and structure. I was unaware at the time that the training I was about to receive would not only improve my interpersonal skills but also prepare me for battle. It involved teamwork, communication, empathy, project management, leadership, and conflict resolution. Additionally, I developed strong interpersonal skills, including conflict resolution, project management, team performance analysis, leadership training, and HR management. You learn more than just how to fight in the Army. You can become more than just a man who can get a woman pregnant, get hard, or provide for others. It teaches you how to develop into a fully realized individual. I was joining something bigger than myself, something that promised some stability, some direction, and some order, rather than merely joining the Army. At the time, I was unable to comprehend that the training I was about to receive would develop my leadership and project management skills, improve my communication skills, help me become more empathetic when handling other people's problems, foster teamwork, and build my conflict resolution abilities.

Additionally, I will enhance my people skills by developing technical and interpersonal skills in conflict mediation, team performance data analysis, project management, HR management, and leadership training. The Army could transform you into a man who is more than just a provider,. Teaches you how to develop personally.

I was entering something greater than myself—something that promised direction, stability, and structure—rather than merely joining the military. I had no idea at the time that the discipline I would acquire would one day save me—not just on the battlefield but also in my thoughts. And give me life skills. A member of the 13B Cannon Crew is indeed a combat soldier. We support frontline troops with 155mm self-propelled or towed artillery systems that fire enormous howitzers. For infantry and armored units, we provide indirect fire, load charges, and set fuses. It's power, pressure, and accuracy. We were the ones who kept the crown of artillery, which they refer to as the "King of Battle," sharp.

I learned what it meant to be a soldier in Hawaii, where I served my first duty station. I served with men of all backgrounds, including academics, alcoholics, racists, intellectuals, and combatants. We were all assigned to the same task: protecting the country. And I threw myself into it.

However, the Army revealed aspects of me that I was unaware existed, in addition to teaching me how to operate a weapon and command a squad. I became aware of my propensity to cheat—just in relationships—at some point during that period. Part curiosity, part survival, that pattern had taken root in my early years and followed me like a shadow into adulthood. It wasn't until I was forty years old that I realized I had a problem.

My first involvement was with my friend's wife back in Detroit. I was twenty years old. To pick him up for a baseball game, I recall pulling up to their house. She was older, and we were both married. She seemed to have a plan when she opened the door, as if she had started something before, I even knocked.

Things rapidly got out of hand.

Before her husband arrived home, we were on the couch. She then asked me to enter the bedroom. Without hesitation or thought, it all happened quickly, like sliding into a base. Just a man and a woman having sex—no feeling, no love. It didn't feel wrong at the time. That was my level of numbness. Regular, casual, disconnected sex had begun to feel like that.

It had nothing to do with the connection. It had to do with getting away. A solution to a gap I had not yet been able to identify.

For years, that cycle continued. I had been conditioned by trauma to keep love and sex apart. For me, it turned into a short-term high that covered up deeper wounds—a quick fix for validation. That kind of behavior wasn't particularly surprising in the military; in some quarters, it was practically expected.

I never used drugs, and I never smoked. Yes, I drank, but women? My vice was that.

Women of all races and backgrounds have always captivated me. God had molded them with grace, beauty, and strength, and there was something divine about them. I didn't always express what I was thinking; most of the time, I let my eyes speak for me, and occasionally, they said more than was necessary.

This is My New Foundation

That wound remained with me even as I advanced through the ranks, honored and respected. Beneath the titles and medals was a boy who was still recovering.

Perhaps it began when you were a kid. I had buried the deep and enduring impression that the older women I had met at such a young age had left in my memory. In the process, I acquired a radar-an instinct. I could tell when a relationship was broken and when someone wasn't being faithful. That gift became a curse, even though I didn't ask for it. It influenced the way I lived, as I constantly sought an unidentified, unfulfilled need.

Although discipline wasn't always evident in my life, as I grew older, I established a personal code for myself. I would never touch a friend's wife or have sex with a woman after meeting her husband. Something within me, shaped by the wound, was still able to distinguish between damage and desire. I made an effort not to hurt anyone.

It was never about love or conquest, in my opinion. It was only sex—a brief reprieve, a peaceful moment to block out the clamor inside of me. I dedicated 26 years of my life to the Army, 13 of which were spent on active duty and the remaining 13 in the reserves. I didn't merely serve during that time; I changed.

This is My New Foundation

From my beginnings as a 13B in nuclear weapons, my journey became more intricate and in-depth. My position as a DAS3 Mainframe Repairman immersed me in the complex inner workings of Decentralized Automated Service Systems, where patience and accuracy were essential. After mastering the 74F Programmer MOS, I went on to command-level automation and systems architecture before switching to the military occupational specialty for information technology specialists, 25B. After gaining experience managing IT operations as a 25Z, I was promoted to 251A Warrant Officer with a focus on information services technology.

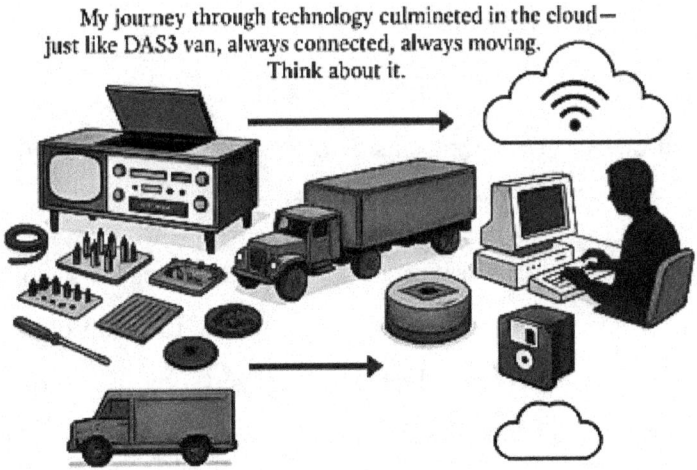

My journey through technology culmineted in the cloud— just like DAS3 van, always connected, always moving. Think about it.

I maxed outboards because I was constantly seeking knowledge, not because I was chasing ribbons. Late nights of studying, early mornings of training others, and an unwavering desire to expand my knowledge were the reasons behind every rank I earned. At West Point, I shaped the Army's future leaders by instructing cadets, but I never stopped learning. That desire to grow began in childhood. I was the child who disassembled TVs and radios to learn how they operated. Once written off as a diversion, that same curiosity turned into my greatest asset.

I've always believed that God has had a profound influence on my life. I believe my mother could see it even when I couldn't. Even when I was careless, she saw something protected in me. She said, "You're one of those people who could fall into a pile of shit and still come out of it smelling like a rose," after I had gotten myself into trouble one day. And I'm going to beat your ass for precisely that reason.

I cried because something inside of me knew it was true, not because of what she said. I didn't fully understand it at the time.

Years later, though, I realized. I was broken and barely making ends meet one day. I signed contract worth a million dollars the next day. Such a change? That is God; it is not a coincidence. He alone has the power to transform brokenness into testimony, scarcity into abundance, and fear into purpose. I also know that God did it so that I could give back, bless others, and live as a living example of what grace can accomplish, not just for me.

"God gave you money so you could give it to me," my first wife would joke. And that might have been true. I gave her money for forty years, even after she remarried. She was the mother of my children, so I wanted her to be alright—not because I had to. I wanted her to be happy even if we couldn't work it out.

In retrospect, I see that I wanted all the women in my life to be content. That was the unseen burden I carried, the shadow of my trauma. Childhood experiences and interactions with older women had conditioned me to be a people-pleaser before I even knew what it meant. I buried all of that deep in my heart and mind for decades.

Right up until COVID-19.

At last, the silence ended. Both the world and I paused. I had to sit with myself, my past, and Everything I believed I had outrun for the first time. I was constantly searching for the next thing—not because I was restless, but because I had a purpose. My rank gave me responsibility, and learning kept me sharp. With every advancement, I gained a broader perspective on how to lead with both technical accuracy and emotional intelligence, as well as how to create systems, train employees, and follow instructions. I had the tools from the Army, but my determination made them into something more.

For me, serving others was never just a job; it was a mission and a calling. It taught me how to combine innovation and discipline, where tradition and change coexist. Like technology, I changed with it. Whether I was wearing a uniform or not, I was constantly creating, reflecting, and striving for more. That is my legacy—not just of service but of influence as well.

However, the Army also instilled in me disillusionment, in addition to structure and skills. I became aware of the flaws, including the racial bias, the covert hypocrisy, and the way politics could eclipse merit. You can be a rising star one day and a threat the next. I recall being chosen for a promotion to Sergeant First Class, which was below my zone. "You haven't been in the Army long enough to make a mistake," the post-sergeant major said, looking me in the eye rather than congratulating me.

He was unable to comprehend how I had gotten up so quickly, but I had. I worked harder than anyone else. When my mother referred to me as a rose, I at last realized what she meant. I continued to rise no matter what I fell into. I continued to develop. That was intentionality, not chance.

However, success came at a cost: loneliness, suspicion, and resentment. I was no longer "just one of the guys." As a Black man, I moved too quickly for some people to find comfort.

Nevertheless, I continued. I created software, built networks, fixed systems that people didn't even realize were broken and recovered data that no one else could.

The Army eventually began to feel small—not because I had outgrown it, but rather because people were attempting to confine me. Their vision, not mine, was what constrained me.

I realized that this chapter was coming to an end at that point.

Even as a child, I was learning the language of survival—reading danger, adapting, hiding. But I didn't yet know how much those skills would cost me.

CHAPTER 4
MILITARY MENTORS
From the Shadows of COVID

Chapter 4:

From the Shadows of COVID-19

No one makes it through the military alone. The uniforms may look the same, but it's the people wearing them who define your experience. They shape your growth, challenge your thinking, and sharpen your purpose.

For me, that journey was guided by five key mentors-men whose leadership, integrity, and quiet strength left a deeper mark on me than any ribbon or promotion ever could. Each taught me something unique, and over time, I wove those lessons into the fabric of who I became. Their influence didn't just guide my career; it helped shape my character.

First, there was First Sergeant Tidwell. He was the bedrock-the first to teach me the truth about military life: one day you're a hero; the next, you're on KP duty. I'll never forget the time I denied the post commander access to a field prop because he didn't know the password of the day. I stood my ground. Later, the general praised me for my discipline, but that same afternoon, I made a mistake and was assigned to kitchen patrol (KP).

When I came back from KP, Tidwell looked me straight in the eye and said, "You can be a goat one minute and a hero the

This is My New Foundation

next-but it all balances out. You're still a soldier." That stuck with me: consistency over perfection. Always.

Now, in popular culture, "GOAT" means Greatest of All Time. But in the military, it's more nuanced. At West Point, the "goat" is the graduate who finishes at the bottom of the class academically. Yet even that title carries a strange kind of respect. In other corners of the Army, the goat is a mascot-a symbol of grit, stubbornness, and the refusal to quit.

Maybe that's why some of the best leaders I encountered weren't the most polished or decorated; they were the most persistent. They didn't leave a legacy through awards-they left it through impact, through lives changed, including mine.

Command Sergeant Major Tidwell was one of them-a Vietnam veteran who survived four tours in the jungle. He wasn't chasing medals; he was focused on training soldiers for war. He knew his purpose, and he lived it. Over the years, he rose through the ranks to become a Command Sergeant Major. Ironically, he would later go on to lead the Signal Brigade in Hawaii, the very branch I would spend the next 22 years of my career in. I didn't know it then, but men like him had already cleared the road I walked in uniform.

He wasn't just a mentor; he was a mirror of the soldier I was becoming.

Lieutenant P was a different kind of leader: sharp, humble, and full of quiet confidence. We were the same age, but I was just a private when he selected me for special weapons duty. Curious, I asked him why. He smiled and said, "Some of your ASVAB scores are higher than mine-and I graduated number one from West Point."

That moment changed my understanding of leadership. His honesty and vulnerability weren't signs of weakness; they were hallmarks of strength. In a world where rank often masked ego or fear, he led with authenticity, and that stuck with me.

Years later, our paths crossed again-both of us now at West Point. I was serving as an instructor, and he had just come back from Harvard as an associate professor. Different titles, different missions, but the same humility. It reminded me that real leaders never stop learning-and they never stop serving.

Lieutenant P wasn't a hands-off officer; he was fully engaged. His section was responsible for the Fire Direction Center (FDC), a critical hub in field artillery that processes and transmits mission data for targeting. In that section was a soldier we all recognized as exceptional— he had the rare skill to execute FDC fire missions entirely on his own, allowing the rest of the team to rest. P didn't take that for granted. Every morning, he'd bring that soldier water and breakfast—not because it was expected, but because he believed in honoring

This is My New Foundation

talent and effort. He understood that leadership sometimes looks like service. He wasn't too proud to support the ones he led.

That's what set him apart. Rank never made him untouchable; service made him unforgettable.

Captain Jackson was a Black officer whose writing was so sharp that even colonels came to him for edits. But it wasn't just his intellect; it was his loyalty. He traveled with his mother to every duty station-quiet, powerful, and unapologetically devoted. That kind of grace isn't taught; it's lived. I don't know how far he rose in rank, but I know he went far in life. He was that rare combination: disciplined, articulate, and grounded in something deeper than ambition.

This is My New Foundation

Sergeant First Class Turner taught me how to listen-literally. He wore a hearing aid, and if someone came to him with nonsense, he'd turn it down and make you repeat your story-this time, short and to the point. But he wasn't just clever; he cared. He asked me what I did on weekends-not for gossip, but to understand me. He sent me to the promotion board in 1985. I maxed it, getting 200 points. He never said "good job"; he just nodded. He didn't need to say it-I already knew.

Active Duty Sergeant First Class (SFC) is the first of the U.S. Army enlisted ranks in which promotion and selection is regulated and effected by the Department of the Army—rather than by local unit commanders. In 1988, when I was selective SFC, I called Turner to tell him the Sergeant Major didn't even congratulate me. He just said, "I don't understand why you got selected below the zone." Turner didn't miss a beat. "Now you're competing with the white boys," he said. "Everything you do from here on out will be scrutinized." Not bitter-just truth. He understood what I was up against, what we were all up against.

Colonel Grubbs-later General Grubbs-was my first-line supervisor at West Point. I met his wife, Judy, first, not even realizing who she was. I helped her with computer work after hours. When Grubbs found out, he said, "You don't have to help my wife." I laughed and replied, "Didn't know she was

This is My New Foundation

your wife, sir." That kind of honesty built a bond.

Grubbs saw something in me-beyond rank, beyond race. He once told me, "People don't listen to your message; they're listening for your mistakes. So slow down. Pronounce every word." Then he added, "White is a state of mind. If you want to study white, look at Bryant Gumbel. That man's whiter than I'll ever be-and they love him for it." That wasn't an insult; it was wisdom. Learn how the world sees you-and use it to your advantage.

Grubbs was more than a commander; he was a mentor, a father figure. From 1988 to now, he's stayed in my life-not for duty, but out of respect. That's rare. That's real.

In 1994, I made the decision to move to the Army Reserve and took a GS position at West Point. This was a transition but it gave me two opportunity one to see my daughters once a month on a steady rotation. And secondly it gave me the opportunity to continue work C&ME as a computer specialist. This department had more technology and there was still a lot to learn. UNIX, networks, robotics, stress analysis application, fiber research, and AutoCAD.

And finally, there was LTC Spearman-Mississippi-born, cool under pressure, always two steps ahead. We served together in the Reserves between Michigan and North Carolina. Since 1994, that connection evolved into something much more than a professional relationship. It became a foundation of mutual respect, trust, and eventually, something that felt like family. Every time I showed up for drill, I came prepared-with a plan not just for myself, but for the soldiers I was responsible for. I believed in readiness and leadership through action. He once said to me, "Where were you when I was on active duty?" That simple line? It meant everything. In that moment, it said, "I see you." And sometimes, that's all a soldier needs—not praise, not medals—just someone who sees them. A mentor.

When Lieutenant Colonel Spearman transitioned to Charlotte under the 108th Division, he didn't forget about me. He remembered the manpower application I had built back at West Point-something I gave freely to the Army, the 70th Division, and units all across the Continental United States.

This is My New Foundation

It wasn't just software; it was a game-changer. With a few clicks, my application could analyze a unit's readiness in under a minute. It provided a real-time SWOT breakdown-Strengths, Weaknesses, Opportunities, and Threats-on each soldier: who was mission-ready, who needed training, who could deploy, and who couldn't.

It gave commanders clarity before they even stepped into a briefing room. And LTC Spearman never forgot that.

He reached back and brought me with him-as Information Systems Chief. Not because I asked, but because my work spoke for itself.

When the 70th Division was deactivated, I found myself in limbo—caught between a chapter I had closed and the next one that hadn't yet opened. I needed a new unit to complete my service. That's when the phone rang. It was LTC Spearman.

There wasn't much to think about. "Absolutely," I said.

I booked a flight and arrived in Charlotte on Memorial Day weekend, 1997. It was a time of transition for me-not just in uniform, but personally. I was used to movement-relocation, adjustment, hitting the ground running. But this time felt different. I was stepping into an unfamiliar unit, in a new city, with a blank slate.

This is My New Foundation

That's the thing about service: you learn to walk into the unknown with your boots laced tight and your head held high.

When I landed, I didn't have a hotel reservation. Back then, you didn't really need one; most cities had rooms available. I figured I'd hit the Holiday Inn and settle in for the night.

But the moment I stepped into the lobby, I knew something was off.

The place was packed-not with families or business travelers, but with NASCAR fans. Memorial Day. Race weekend. Charlotte.

The energy was wild-loud music, beer vendors, people in racing jackets. The clerk looked up at me with a tired smile. "You know what weekend this is?" she asked.

"Memorial Day weekend," I said.

She laughed. "It's also race weekend. And no, we don't have any rooms."

Just as I was about to turn around, a woman stepped out from the back office. She had quiet authority. "Are you a soldier?" she asked.

"Yes, ma'am."

Without hesitation, she said, "Then we have a room for you."

This is My New Foundation

In that moment, I remembered that even in chaos, service still carries respect.

The next morning, I was up early. While the city slept, I was on the road. No introductions, no delays-just systems and silence: DNS, WINs, TCP/IP, servers, and comms. I brought it all online. The unit had a contractor install the server room, but the contractor did not setup everything and I brought the network alive.

By afternoon, as the soldiers returned from lunch, everything was running like clockwork. I didn't say much; I didn't have to. The work spoke for itself.

A few days later, I got the call: "Would you consider taking a permanent job down here in Charlotte?"

That weekend started in chaos-but ended in purpose. And it all began with a simple question:

"Are you a soldier?"

When I first moved to Charlotte, I was what some might call home-challenged. Honestly, I was embarrassed. My credit had taken a serious hit after leaving active duty. I ended up living at the InTown Suites for nearly two years, quietly working to rebuild my financial life. Every paycheck, every extra dollar went toward paying off the debts I owed—one by one. I remember the day they repossessed my car after I missed a few payments. That stung.

The only thing I stayed current on was my child support—and I paid that directly to my daughter's mother, no court involved. I took pride in that, even when the rest of my life felt like it was slipping. Without God, I don't believe I would've had the strength to endure that transition. It was a storm I wouldn't wish on anyone, but one that taught me the value of humility, discipline, and faith.

I didn't have much, but I made sure to face everything I owed. I didn't file bankruptcy. I didn't run. I paid every credit card, loan, and unpaid bill that had followed me from my military life into civilian reality. Some nights, I had to choose between food and dignity—and I chose dignity. I told myself, "You started this. You'll finish it".

And that became a kind of spiritual practice—owning my mess, quietly cleaning it up, and trusting that there was more ahead than just this motel room and overdue notices.

During that season, I found myself in church most Sundays. I didn't go to be seen. I didn't go to meet people. I went because I needed something steady. I'd sit in the back row, say nothing, and listen. I paid my tithes faithfully, even when it felt like I couldn't afford to. I gave not because I was trying to buy a blessing, but because I needed to stay connected to something beyond survival.

I needed the Word, but I wasn't ready for community. I was still wrestling with shame, with silence, with holding it all together. That was my way of surviving—stay quiet, stay low, and let the healing come in small pieces. Each sermon gave me just enough fuel to get through the week.

Financial recovery wasn't just about money. It was about reclaiming my self-worth, one sacrifice at a time. It was about facing what I didn't want to admit—that I'd let some things fall apart because I was tired, or stubborn, or lost. But through it all, I stayed grounded in faith.

God didn't rescue me with a sudden miracle. He walked beside me through the grind—step by step—teaching, shaping, and guiding me with each hardship, preparing me for something greater: my grandchildren.

That's where I found my true foundation—not in a credit score, a car, or even a home, but in the unwavering decision to rise, again and again, no matter how many times life knocked me down.

From fists to fear, and then to fire—my childhood trauma became a furnace that would shape my adult decisions, for better or worse.

This is My New Foundation

Chapter 5:

A Reunion to Remember Honoring the Past Before Everything Changed

Some memories become more vivid over time rather than fading because of what they meant, not because of what we did.

In 2019, I was back home visiting my brother—something I often did when I needed to reconnect and feel grounded. During that visit, my brother Money and I decided to attend a worship service at my friend Tyrone Brooks' church. The room was filled with music—soul-stirring, powerful worship that reached deep into the spirit.

As I sat there, immersed in the sound and sacred energy of that space, something urged me to look up.

And that's when I saw it—an angel.

Right there in front of me.

The moment was too profound to keep to myself. I stood up and shared what I was seeing with the congregation. To my amazement, I wasn't alone—others said they saw it too.

We were all overcome. The room became still, holy. It felt like a divine visitation, a sign of reassurance and hope. And looking back, that moment holds even more weight—because just a few months later, the world would be shaken by the pandemic.

But in that moment, we were reminded of something eternal: we are never alone. Heaven is always closer than we think.

Later that year I had a silent feeling in the summer of 2019 that it was time to bring people home. With my childhood friends, I planned a neighborhood reunion that brought generations together rather than just having a backyard barbecue. For those who grew up in Detroit's 7 Mile to 8 Mile neighborhood—Greenfield to Southfield—a neighborhood rich in Black homeownership, tenacity, and civic pride, this was a hallowed return. We extended an invitation to everyone who has influenced those streets, including newcomers and longtime neighbors; we came to reconnect, not just to remember.

Honoring the past was more important than reliving it. It had to do with legacy.

After 26 years in the service, I had recently retired. I had led troops, served all around the world, and launched a company from scratch. Rapier Solutions, a company that provides information technology services, supports a wide range of project management specialties. But Detroit never abandoned me, no matter how far I went. The heartbeat, the code, and the grit were all a part of me. I had a duty to it. Thanks, I owed it.

This is My New Foundation

Detroit was tough in the 1970s, but it had a strong foundation. You were a part of a block and a tribe, not simply a house. Your mother was notified before you arrived home if you misbehaved at school since your neighbor had already called her. The White Pages carried accountability in addition to numbers.

In every way, the reunion that summer seemed like a homecoming. Childhood faces—now grandparents, uncles, and elders—laughed, wept, and cuddled as if no time had passed. Under the warm Michigan sun, we shared experiences and reassured one another that we were alive. We remained here. Standing.

It was peaceful. It was therapeutic.

The mayor even paid attention. A minor but significant reminder that what we had created was important was the letter of recognition that my buddies Angel and Jenel and the team received.

However, none of us anticipated how brief that tranquility would be. Six months later, COVID-19 spread like wildfire through our neighborhoods. The virus did not simply impact our city; it destroyed it. That reunion's fifty attendees would no longer be there. Fifty. I would never be hugged again by the same arms that had embraced me that summer. Those who had laughed would stop talking.

This is My New Foundation

What started as a life celebration turned into a farewell.

And as a custodian of that moment, as well as a man, I felt it profoundly. It was heartbreak, not just grief.

They were humans, not simply figures flickering on the cable news screen. My people. Names and faces that once brought discipline, fun, and direction into my life. The same people who shaped me in those early adolescent years. They were tales, sacrifices, and steady hands, not numbers.

These were the individuals who transformed disorder into order and caring into correction. I learned from them how to conduct myself, how to work honorably, and how to arrive on time and with a purpose. They set an example of responsibility, deference, and pride in hard work. Sometimes, they used words to impart their knowledge, and at other times, they used glances that conveyed a great deal of information.

They helped me become a contributing member of society. They shaped my work ethic in real-time by setting an example rather than giving lectures. I discovered that it was important to show up. That effort was important. That persona encompassed not only your public persona but also your private self. Aside from farmers, auto workers are some of the hardest-working people in America.

And I wasn't present to bid them farewell. It still hurts.

I was attempting to cling to the memory of a joy we never thought would be our last when I was in North Carolina, miles away from the place where I was raised.

Here in the South, my wife's family turned into a haven. I'm always thankful for them. You can feel alone even while you're in love, though. Sometimes, only those who have experienced your tale can truly comprehend your silence, as grief has its language. It doesn't necessarily express itself through sobs or breakdowns. It can occasionally be heard through restless nights, constricted chests, faraway gazes, or the silent anguish of memories you can't share with anybody.

Each of us uniquely experiences grief. Some people experience it as a sudden, overwhelming, and unavoidable tidal wave. Others experience it gradually, weaving itself into their everyday lives like an enduring shadow. There is no set of guidelines, no guidebook, and no proper way to grieve. That's why it's often misinterpreted and alienating.

I have discovered that compassion is not an innate quality. It is constructed gradually, loss by loss, brick by brick. It develops when you have experienced your brokenness and sat in quiet in agony, realizing that you lack the words to mend it. Because they haven't had to deal with it, a lot of people don't comprehend grief. Not quite yet.

This is My New Foundation

Calls were revered. Group texts turned into lifelines. Despite the pain, we kept checking on each other. There were too many cuts, and each new loss was a new one.

I relied on the discipline, organization, and poise I had learned in the Army. But that wasn't enough to keep me from being sad. Even that was unable to prepare me for the helplessness of not being able to show up, hold someone's hand, or grieve appropriately, as well as the shame of being gone.

I followed Detroit's instructions. I arrived in spirit. I provided remote assistance and took the lead when necessary. I reminded our people that care, not proximity, is what defines a community. We created unshakable relationships on those streets through joy, hardship, and shared survival.

A few names to keep in mind from the list of COVID-19 victims are Put some name here.

I got Everything from Detroit.

We also gave back to the city where we grew up, to the future generation, and each other in the summer of 2019. Although it might have been our final moment together, with laughter resonating through well-known neighborhoods, we will always be remembered. Every life we touched and every tale that is still being told bears witness to that moment, that unity, and that love.

This is My New Foundation

Visit our archives if you'd like:

https://www.facebook.com/groups/2439314816081568/

Each time I buried a piece of pain, I planted a root. What I didn't realize then was that those roots would grow into something I could not ignore.

CHAPTER 6
ADVENTURES ABROAD, REFLECTIONS WITHIN
A Beautiful Escape from the Weight of Memory

Chapter 6:

A Beautiful Escape from the Weight of Memory

This section While some people travel to explore, others do so to escape. Me? Traveling helps me remember who I am, and occasionally, it helps me forget who I was. I wanted the room to breathe, to think, to recover aspects of myself that had been buried beneath duty and survival after Everything I had been through, including a chaotic childhood, years spent in uniform, and the crazy rollercoaster that is entrepreneurship. Sometimes, that place was located halfway around the world rather than in treatment or isolation.

The streets of Rome have a hallowed quality about them. Amid ruins and tenacity, I sensed a connection to something eternal. Instead of feeling insignificant, I felt visible as I stood where emperors had once stood. "You, too, are built to last," the tenacity of that ancient city seemed to whisper. It was even more impactful when I shared it with my wife. Rome was more than just a place we visited; it was the most romantic location mt wife and I had ever been to. Time seemed to want us to appreciate each moment, so it slowed down.

Even the silence felt like song as we floated along the canals of Venice. Venice is a dream floating on water, not merely a city. I wasn't a CEO, a veteran, or a man with too many memories to mention in that dream. I was just a man at peace, a husband, and a lover.

Greek, Roman, Arab, and Norman cultures all blended to create something intricate and magnificent in Sicily, showcasing the beauty of collision. Like me: a tale that is difficult to describe.

We visited the Godfather house in Sicily—the one where Michael Corleone looks out the window just before witnessing the car explosion that kills his wife. A wedding was taking place just a in few hours, yet the caretaker still took the time to give us a tour. As I looked out the windows, taking it all in, I couldn't help but think that only in America can someone come from the inner city of Detroit and one day find themselves standing in a scene straight out of a legendary film. What a joy. What a journey.

Next was Iceland. Chilly. Untamed and fierce. The first location I went to where nature didn't give a damn about my identity. The sound of the waterfalls was louder than my thoughts. God seemed to be saying, "You're still here," as the sky glowed in a glorious exhibition. I still own you. The portions of me that had withstood both fire and ice—the parts that were still growing and healing—were reflected in the black sand beaches, volcanic plains, and eerie glacier silence.

This is My New Foundation

I have experienced the rhythmic soul of Havana, gazed at Croatia's medieval walls of a castle, I was a big Game of Thrones fan. My wife Hazel and I visit Dubrovnik, which served as the primary stand-in for King's Landing. Hazel and I strolled through the royal hallways of London. Every location made its mark. Each served as a reminder that life is more than just suffering. That happiness is waiting, not just potential.

Cuba was like entering a time-stamped image. I was reminded of Detroit by the vehicles, the music, and the spirit of survival—beautiful, worn, and proud.

I felt the old whispers riding the wind as I stood on the shores of Lake Titicaca in Peru. Every anecdote made you wonder how we walked Machu Picchu. Then you question how humans continue to return here even though 1,000 people die here each year. As I watched life unfold on the reed-woven floating islands, I realized that—like myself—humans can create stability even atop the most unstable foundations.

I still smile when I think of one moment in Peru. I observed a local dancer who had the same face and body as my sister-in-law, Sibby. In the finest way possible, it took me by surprise. "There's always someone who looks like someone you love, no matter where you go," I thought. I was reminded of how exquisitely interconnected we are all in that moment.

This is My New Foundation

The Amazon River humbled me. It served as a reminder that there are still areas where nature is in control and people are only visitors, not kings. I felt small again in its enormity but somehow entire at the same time. Our men group Hurly, Travis and John discovered something remarkable—a nightclub in the middle of the rainforest—just when I thought I had the jungle figured out. Locals danced with a wild, unbridled excitement as lights flared against the leaves and music throbbed through the woods like a heartbeat. I was swaying to Michael Jackson's beat one minute and amazed at the ancient silence the next. It was electric and bizarre, proving that celebration can occur even in the wildest places on earth.

I have been all around the United States back home, from Savannah's beauty to New Orleans' soul. I've gone hunting in Mississippi, stopped in Bluefield, West Virginia, the hometown of my wife Hazel, and stayed at The Greenbrier, a place where luxury and American history collide.

We've rolled through Beverly Hills in a car that forced a stranger to give us a tour of opulent properties, assuming we were mansion buyers, that was a laugh and driven through the autumn fire in Vermont and the hallowed grounds of Gettysburg. I still find that funny.

From the western legend of Dodge City to the deer-lined highways of Connecticut, my journey has been as wild as it has been wide. I've experienced life from beginning to end.

Travel evolved into more than just a means of healing during this time. It turned into a statement: I'm still developing. Because I brought myself with me wherever I went. And gradually, in every new setting, I released weights I was unaware I still carried.

COVID-19 affected my mental health. I became paranoid, reclusive, and fearful as a result. However, the window was busted open by transit. It served as a reminder that life is about more than just surviving worry.

This is My New Foundation

It served as a reminder that there is life—real life—beyond suffering. And that delight becomes holy when it is sought with purpose.

Antarctica and Easter Island are still destinations I'd want to visit. They will remind me that I am still capable of amazement, not because they will complete me.

Perhaps that is the true focus of this chapter:

Awakening to ponder.

Getting your happiness back.

And discovering fragments of your soul strewn all across the globe, awaiting your return home.

Leaving home wasn't freedom. It was relocation. The ghosts didn't stay behind—they traveled with me, even into uniform

This is My New Foundation

CHAPTER 7
THE ONSET OF THE STORM
When the World Changed— and So Did I

Chapter 7:

The Onset of the Storm
When the World Changed—and So Did I

I had witnessed all the conflicts, betrayals, and crushing strains of leadership before the COVID-19 pandemic. However, nothing could have prepared me for the impending unseen storm. There was no gunshot to avoid, no battlefield to outmaneuver, and no difficulty to outwork. Through the glare of a computer or the breath of strangers, this storm came silently and brought the planet to its knees.

Fifty individuals. We lost that many people at the summer reunion, which I had planned to honor life, community, and roots while reestablishing ties with my former neighborhood. Fifty neighbors, friends, and family members. Lost.

The calls came one by one. The written word. The headlines. Until all of a sudden, it was a personal catastrophe rather than merely a worldwide one. Very intimate. Now, the happiness we had documented in that July get-together felt like a snapshot from a different era—a final giggle, a final embrace, a final opportunity.

And I shut down along with the world. I initially convinced myself that I was being prudent, responsible, and cautious. In actuality, though, I was terrified in a manner I hadn't experienced since I was a young child, attempting to hide behind blankets and block out the noise around me.

A preoccupation developed out of the dread of germs. I had trouble breathing in public places. In my own house, I was unable to remain motionless. Every cough seemed like an alert; every surface was dangerous. I was attempting to survive an invisible foe, not just to keep safe.

However, isolation posed a greater threat to me than the COVID-19 virus.

I had managed to keep my PTSD under control for years. I was able to control the darkness in my head thanks to military training, structure, and purpose. But the leash broke during lockdown. My home's walls turned into a cell's walls, and I was imprisoned there by memories I had escaped for my entire life.

In my mind, it was like being a prisoner of war.

The pattern I depended on disappeared. Reunions ceased, the office closed, and the gym shuttered. I was left in stillness without those pillars, and when your past is loud, silence can be deafening.

I began to fall apart.

Slowly but steadily, paranoia began to creep in. I started to perceive danger where none existed. My wife's family, which had become my own, began to seem alien. I saw silence as rejection, smiles as condemnation, and side remarks as betrayals. It was trauma that twisted Everything into survival mode, not reality.

The statements of one sister-in-law, in particular, hurt the most. Not only did she say it, but people seemed to believe it with ease. She had been homeless when I assisted her. I had provided for her kids. However, it seemed as though Everything vanished as mistrust and anxiety took hold. The gossip rewrote love. The rumor was I had changed.

That was painful.

Even now, my wife's family has never questioned me about what went wrong or why I became so reserved. Nevertheless, I was there for them while they were in the hospital, dealing with family issues, or even experiencing homelessness. I showed up, I gave, and I cared without hesitation. Their silence, however, spoke more than words when it was my turn to be hurt. Five years have passed, and nobody has inquired, "Are you okay?" I occasionally ponder whether it was because I stopped paying for dinners, trips, and holidays and started to focus only on my grandchildren. I'm not sure whether they or I caused the distance. All I know is that I try to help those I care about when they are in pain. I inquire. I make an effort to comprehend. That they never really cared until I became a resource to improve their lives may be what hurts the most. Nevertheless, I have no hard feelings. I wish everyone the best.

The most challenging aspect, though, was seeing my marriage withstand the strain of Everything. The lady I had been with for twenty-six years—my sanctuary, my ride-or-die—was caught in the middle. We also bent more than we ought to have, even if we never broke. Between us, the stress, the quiet, and the loneliness piled up like bricks. On certain evenings, I considered leaving. Not out of rage, but simply from plain tiredness. Because I thought that perhaps I was simply too damaged to be loved at the moment.

The financial situation also collapsed. The company that I had worked so hard to build—Rapier Solutions—began to crumble beneath the weight of a world that was no longer working. Staff morale plummeted, contracts dried up, and the pressure of leadership became too much to bear. I made an effort to protect my colleagues and make the proper decisions. But the debt increased with each choice. I soon found myself bearing a load that I had not requested but was unable to ignore.

I believed that I was failing as a husband, parent, friend, and leader.

Nevertheless, I managed to continue breathing.

I kept waking up somehow.

This is My New Foundation

Because there was a whisper inside of me that would not die, even in the deepest recesses of this storm, this isn't the end, a whisper said.

Before the breakthrough, this is the breaking.

For anything new to grow, this is the peeling away.

I was being remade, even though I was unaware of it at the time.

> Not ruined.
>
> Not removed.
>
> But changed.
>
> Even if the storm almost drowned me, it was only the beginning.

So I started writing. I began researching why those who are neglected as children frequently develop into strong-willed men who speak little. To understand how trauma affects human behavior and our sense of security, I thoroughly examined Maslow's Theory of Human Motivation and the concept of hypervigilance—two separate yet intricately related ideas. I started to discover who I was during that process. I began to see the facets of my identity and the reasons behind them. I was even able to see why her sister had once referred to me as a "know-it-all." I've come to realize over time that I'm neither superior nor more intelligent than anyone else. However, I am passionate about what I know and what I think is real. And I understand that as I continue to learn, even my understanding of the truth may change day by day.

Her sister once turned to me in the car and said, "I didn't know you were featured in Technology magazine," and then, "And that you made the Inc. 5000 list."

You didn't know, of course—I thought to myself, because you never really knew me. To my sister-in-law, I was just her sister's husband. That was the extent of her curiosity. She never wanted to see beyond the label. And honestly, that's where the misunderstandings in our relationship began.

The truth is, most people have no idea who they're talking to—or what they might learn if they truly listened. We close our minds not because we cannot understand, but because it helps preserve the version of reality we've already decided to believe.

https://www.inc.com/magazine/201409/darren-dahl/inc.500-rapier-solutions-william-bailey-running-a-company-based-on-military-ideals.html

https://www.itworldcanada.com/article/microsoft-widens-role-of-windows-storage-server/21472

The military gave me rules, structure, a new identity. But beneath the medals and missions, the wounded boy never stopped watching.

105

Chapter 8:

The Battle of My Mind vs Reality
Confronting the Invisible War Within

God Whispered Back When the Silence grew loud.

The most difficult conflicts do not take place on battlefields. They are battled in sick beds, in deserted rooms, and on restless evenings when the only sound is your breathing, which is difficult enough. They are waged in the quiet between ideas and the reverberation of unclear inquiries. At the height of the COVID-19 outbreak, I was caught up in that war. While everything around me was silent, I was disintegrating on the inside.

Before the epidemic, I believed I was strong--not only physically but also psychologically, spiritually, and emotionally. I'd already endured a lot in life, including childhood trauma, military service, failed relationships, and business challenges. I had learned how to compartmentalize grief, push through, and survive. But what I didn't comprehend was that surviving had become my sole means of existence. And when the world came to a halt, when the clamor of business, travel, and distraction faded, I was forced to confront the version of myself that I had avoided for years.

This is My New Foundation

I started to unravel—not with a scream, but with a subtle aching. At first, I assumed it was simply stress. Then, I realized it was something deeper. I was not only fatigued; I was empty. The PTSD I'd had since childhood, the spiritual numbness I'd suppressed, the anxieties I'd ignored--all of it surfaced. It was like standing in a flooded basement that I had kept sealed for decades, and the water was up to my neck.

I had trouble falling asleep. Unable to think clearly. I was no longer able to pray as I once could. And I was afraid of that. My faith had always served as my compass, but all of a sudden, it seemed far away, like a beach, I could see but could never reach.

I joined BetterHelp out of desperation. At first, I kept it a secret. I still carried that old-fashioned stigma, particularly as a soldier and Black man. "Psychotherapy?" Our purpose was not to do that. However, pride was no longer a luxury I could afford. I required assistance. I also needed it quickly.

I will always remember the first time I logged into a virtual session. With my heart racing as if I were about to enter a conflict zone, my fingers hovered over the mouse. My chest was tense, and my palms were sweating. I almost pulled back. However, something within me told me to "stay"—something tenacious, something that was still alive. So I did.

This is My New Foundation

The therapist was patient and composed. She took her time with me. "Tell me why are you here," she stated simply. Then the tears started to fall. Not too loud. Not dramatic. At first, I did not even notice the constant, slow streams. I started talking about my early years, the events that took place behind closed doors, the ladies, the masks, and the numbness. And for the first time, I was speaking to a professional, licensed, and vetted therapists.

—without criticism or disruption.

I will always remember the first time I logged into a virtual session. With my heart pounding as if I were about to enter a conflict zone, my fingers hovered over the mouse. My chest was tense, and my palms were sweating. I almost pulled back. However, something within me told me to "stay"—something tenacious, something that was still alive. So I did.

The surface cracked during just one session. However, I discovered that mending is not a straight line. On some days, I felt lighter; on other days, the burden of recollection weighed heavily on me. I, therefore, contacted the VA, another resource I had shunned. I had always felt disconnected from the Veterans Affairs system, but this time, I made an effort to engage with it. The counselor I spoke with were familiar with military trauma; she understood what it was like to wear the uniform and bring unseen wounds home with them. She had experience with the Fort Jackson community.

The surface cracked during just one session. However, I discovered that healing is not a linear process. On some days, I felt lighter; on other days, the burden of recollection weighed heavily on me. I, therefore, contacted the VA, another resource I had shunned. I had always felt disconnected from the Veterans Affairs system, but this time, I made an effort to engage with it. A doctor I spoke with were familiar with military trauma; they understood what it was like to wear the uniform and bring unseen wounds home with them.

He helped me give words to things I was unable to identify in that one session. He helped me confront what I had suppressed. He also provided me with a roadmap for rebuilding my soul, along with coping mechanisms. He offer me the VA services but I chose to stay with BetterHelp.

They helped me give words to things I was unable to identify. They helped me confront what I had suppressed. They also provided me with a roadmap for rebuilding my soul, along with coping mechanisms.

As the weeks passed, I began to ask God, "What now?" rather than "Why?" My faith started to change at that point. My search for meaning was more important than for miracles.

This is My New Foundation

Small moments, scripture, silence, and forgiveness were where I discovered it.

COVID-19 had taken away my control, my rhythm, and my business. But it also provided me with stillness, something I was unaware I needed. God reassured me in that silence that I was being recreated, not irreparably damaged.

I gave up seeking approval from money. I began gauging achievement in terms of peace rather than contracts. I began reframing my legacy to encompass how I lived each day, not just what I left behind. That insight marked a sea change.

This is My New Foundation

Then, I realized that Detroit was my hometown. My city. My origins. The location taught me to fight with my heart rather than my fists. I reflected on porch conversations and block gatherings and how we supported one another without any justification. I still harbored that grit. It served as a reminder that I was not working alone. Beyond trauma, I had a deeper base. My legacy went beyond suffering.

I, therefore, rebuilt.

Not in a hurry. Not neatly. However, bit by piece.

With the VA and BetterHelp assisting me in discovering my voice.

I am finding my mission with the power of prayer.

With faith assisting me in getting back on my feet.

And I came to the profound realization that my foundation was exposed during the epidemic, not cracked. By God's grace, I was able to rebuild it now, stronger, softer, and wiser.

This is my new foundation.

Not from pride but from the truth.

Not built-in noise, but rather quiet.

Purpose, rather than perfection.

This is My New Foundation

And if I can rebuild after everything I have seen, survived, and done, so can you. You are not too far gone, regardless of the storm you are trekking through. You are not alone. And your recovery might just start in the silence.

Allow it.

Allow the mending to begin--not all at once, but gradually, faithfully, as dawn breaks after a long night.

Allow stillness to do what noise cannot: show what requires your attention rather than your avoidance.

Allow the suffering to speak, but do not allow it to have the last word. Listen to what it is telling you, then let it go. You do not have to carry it indefinitely.

Allow tears to fall if necessary. Let the memories rise if necessary. Allow your heart to break open—only open things can receive.

Let the grace that has been pursuing you finally catch up. Allow it to hold you. Allow it to cover you. Allow it to rebuild you.

Allow faith to return to the heart of your life—not in perfection, but in presence. Taking a breath. In surrender. In truth.

Let forgiveness begin with you. Allow tranquility to become a decision, not merely a sensation.

This is My New Foundation

Allow yourself to let go of who you used to be to become who you are today.

        Allow it all to happen.

        Because it is not the end.

        It is the start of your new foundation.

Some battles are fought in the soul. Others are internal and invisible in the mind. The next chapter of my life would demand a different kind of bravery.

This is My New Foundation

CHAPTER 9

A FUTURE FORGED FROM RESILIENCE

*Turning Setbacks into Strength and
Pain into Purpose*

Chapter 9:

A Future Forged from Resilience
Turning Setbacks into Strength and Pain into Purpose

The world Changed in 2020. And so did I.

At first, it felt like everything I would construct was collapsing: my business, my mental health, my trust in others--even my faith felt distant, like a buddy I had not spoken to in a while. I felt fatigued in ways I could not understand. But then something unexpected occurred.

During the silence... I began to reconstruct. Not because I wanted to or because I had a plan, but because the human spirit, when united with purpose and faith, has a way of finding light even in the darkest tunnel. And that is what I discovered: light, not from outside, but from inside.

Resilience is more than just surviving adversity; it is about thriving in the face of it and using the identical material that sought to break me to make me stronger, wiser, and sharper today. Softer where I need to be.

I started with what I had, not what I would lose.

I embraced my heritage—Detroit. The city where I grew up. The place that showed me how to bounce back from setbacks.

Resilience was not a catchphrase in this place, where community was crucial—it was a matter of life and death. I thought back to those block parties as kids, those neighborhood get-togethers, and how we looked out for each other without permission. I still carried that spirit with me.

I relied on the strength of my hometown even though I was miles away from North Carolina and grieving. It served as a reminder that, despite my progress, I was not alone in my efforts. I belonged to something greater. I had been all along.

I then turned my attention inward, examining my attempts to overlook my mental health, finances, and entanglements.

Loss, loneliness, and disappointing loved ones were three things I had to learn the hard way. COVID-19 revealed flaws in my character, as well as those of my company and our supply chains. But light enters through crevices.

I gave up looking for approval from money. I began to redefine success in terms of my peace rather than my cash account.

I began controlling my mental health instead of avoiding it. What I had considered "soft" or "optional"—therapy, prayer, rest, and boundaries—became crucial to my existence.

I stopped treating my entanglement as an anesthetic for suffering and began to value connection over conquest. I

This is My New Foundation

recognized that intimacy without vulnerability is merely acting, and I was bored of it.

I examined my relationships, particularly the ones that were stressful, and made peace with what I could not change. Some individuals will never see you. Some wounds do not close properly. But this does not mean you stop loving; it simply means you stop attempting to be understood by people who are determined to misunderstand you.

I put more into the individuals who saw me fully and still loved me: my wife, my children, my grandchildren, my spiritual brothers and sisters, and the friends who stayed even when I was not easy to be around.

And I discovered God again—not in a pulpit, not in a neatly crafted sermon, but in the silence. In the quiet of an early walk. During an open and honest therapy session. I received an unexpected call from an old buddy. God appeared amid my mess, not waiting for me to tidy it up.

When I discovered this, I regained my sense of purpose. Not the sort you share online, but the kind that gets you out of bed. The kind that says, "You have not finished yet."

I had another dream, not of wealth or fame but of influence. I wanted my story to have meaning, even though it was dirty, unpleasant, and true. I wanted other survivors, fathers, spouses, entrepreneurs, and veterans to know that they are not alone. You are not insane. It is not too late to fix you.

You are evolving.

And living a healthy, healed, and purpose-driven existence became my new mission. To proclaim truth where there was once quiet.

It must provide a foundation of love, faith, and fortitude—not only for myself but also for the generation that will be watching.

Since they are observing.

And I want them to witness a man who used the fire to brighten the path ahead rather than letting it destroy him.

I have no idea what storms might yet hit. However, I am aware that I have survived the worst of it.

Not the same individual.

However, from a place of greater awareness.

I thought I could outrun the past. I didn't realize I had only given it new uniforms to wear.

CHAPTER 10

THE BLESSING IN THE STORM

Chapter 10:

The Blessing in the Storm

The world seemed to be falling apart. Amid the COVID-19 pandemic, on a Monday morning in November 2020, a few days before Thanksgiving, something happened. Everything was shrouded in fear. Families were being split up, jobs were going missing, and a silent killer was ruthlessly rifling through areas. There was a lot of loss and fear in the air.

Nevertheless, a miracle occurred amid all that gloom.

As usual, I woke up at five in the morning that day. I got on my computer and looked through the internet and the news. After that, I went downstairs to get my glass of orange juice, as I usually do. I checked my NC Cash 5 numbers after I got back up and went to the North Carolina Lottery website, which is now more of a habit than a hope. This was my first peek since Saturday because I hadn't checked the previous day.

However, something was different this time.

I blinked. Then blinked once more. For the third time.

$xxx,xxx.xx

This is My New Foundation

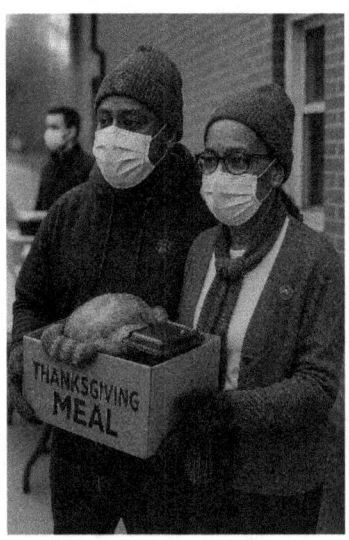

I initially thought the screen was malfunctioning. Hazel had not yet woken up. Returning downstairs, I sat by myself in the kitchen and stared at that number until it finally clicked.

We were victorious. Not enough to give up all and vanish, but more than enough to serve as a reminder that even during the most difficult years, light can still shine.

I told Hazel when she eventually woke up.

Tears rolled into her eyes. We simply held each other while we stood in the corridor. Quiet, overwhelmed thankfulness instead of a raucous celebration.

"Are you serious?" she inquired. "You enjoy playing tricks on people, don't you?"

"I'm serious," I declared. "Check out the website."

She did.

After that, we grinned—not because Everything had been resolved right away, but rather because, for the first time in a long time, we thought perhaps Everything would work out.

We didn't require further items. We didn't require brand-new vehicles or a getaway that was unavailable during a lockdown. We had to do something constructive, something that would lift the burden that COVID-19 had placed on our community.

It dawned on me then: turkeys. Thanksgiving dinners, not just turkeys.

Some families were unable even to consider taking a vacation, let alone afford one. And I knew just where to begin: downtown shelters and our church.

However, I didn't want to work alone. "I need you all to come with me," I stated over the phone to my grandsons. We will bless a few people.

Together, we went shopping, me pushing one cart while they pushed the others. We purchased pies, rolls, cranberry sauce, potatoes, stuffing, and a dozen turkeys. After that, we put up meal boxes that had enough food to nourish a family and lift their spirits.

James, Stephon, and Jamil were there that Wednesday, gloved up and wearing masks, standing next to me as we distributed those meals based on a list that Mrs. Hazel Byard, Hazel's mother, had assisted in compiling. We went from house to house and block to block, delivering Thanksgiving feasts around Charlotte.

I saw my grandsons treat others with respect and care. No cell phones. Avoid any distractions. Only the heart.

I realized then that we were giving out hope rather than just food. The point was that it was never about lottery riches or legacy. Teaching my grandsons that giving has its benefits was the goal. That generosity is strength, not weakness, especially when no one is seeing.

My wife and I stayed inside when the local news arrived since we weren't looking for attention. Interviews were not what we wanted. Attention was not what we wanted. We were not the focus of this. We wanted the boys to be in the picture so they could genuinely experience what it was like to make a difference in someone's life, not just to become famous.

We wanted children to know what it meant to be there for others—not with a critical eye, but with a heart full and a plate warm. And they did. The ride, the goal, and the lesson were the true winners of Thanksgiving, not the check. Sincerity is a decision. A boon. Not a flaw.

Many people nowadays mistakenly equate giving with weakness and believe that compassion can be exploited.

However, my perspective is different. Kindness, in my opinion, is a strength that one chooses to share. In a harsh world, showing kindness requires more bravery than showing coldness. Giving without expecting anything in return requires a strong heart, and it needs knowledge to understand that helping others doesn't take anything away from you.

I wanted my grandkids to learn how to lead with grace, not how to make headlines. Sincerity is perhaps the most powerful gift you can provide. And it's always important.

We also handed $1,000 to each of my nephews and all of our siblings. It was a modest yet loving gesture. The goal was to let people know they weren't forgotten, not to make money.

People wept. Some joined us in prayer. Others only bowed and left in silence, holding their food as if it were precious.

That day was pure in a time when Everything seemed questionable. It served as a reminder of the importance of family, faith, and charitable giving.

We lost a lot to COVID-19. It took away our routines, our mental tranquility, and, for too many, the people we cared about. However, that victory? That unanticipated boon? It returned something to me—the chance to offer. Furthermore, it provided me with the opportunity to teach my grandkids the true meaning of legacy.

What people say about you after you're gone is more important than how much money you leave behind. The majority of us will not be recorded in history books, but we will live on in people's hearts—in the silent tales of a grandfather or grandmother who was kind, who defended others, or who donated when it counted.

I silently drove my grandson home after the last Thanksgiving meal was delivered, and the last "thank you" was spoken through a broken door. My spirit was full, not because I was exhausted, though I was. It was fuller than it had been for ages.

Not only had I benefited others, but something had changed within myself as well. Peace had taken the place of the fear that had once weighed heavily on my chest. The sort that comes from knowing that even if things don't work out, I still have something solid to stand on, rather than the kind that comes from believing that Everything will work out.

Faith. Goal. A fresh Start.

That we still have the option to be kind even when faced with uncertainty. Continue to choose love.

The lotto jackpot was only the spark, never the real blessing. The lesson that giving is the most effective way to recover was a true blessing, reminding us that our hearts don't have to stop when the world stops.

I used to believe that being strong meant being in control and knowing the answers. I now understand that true strength is having the courage to say, "Use me."

And he did.

I didn't merely express gratitude that year; I lived it.

CHAPTER 11

THIS IS MY NEW FOUNDATION

A LIFE REBUILT FROM THE GROUND UP

Chapter 11:

This Is My New Foundation
A Life Rebuilt from the Ground Up

Every journey has a point at which you pause, take stock of your surroundings, and recognize that this is no longer the beginning. This is a very different matter. Something shaped by all you have experienced. Even if you have never been there before, it feels familiar.

My new foundation is this. Not my childhood home. Not the overseas barracks where I slept. Not the workplace where I established my business. Not the places where I tried to conceal myself or impress others.

No, this is an internal foundation. invisible. But sturdy.

I spent most of my life moving like a Man on a mission, yet my feet were never really on the ground. Pain, guilt, failure, and quiet were all things I was always escaping. And sprinting in search of something: serenity, love, success, or a purpose.

However, you cannot escape your past. You must make peace with it. Please keep it in place. God bless it. Instead of it being the conclusion of your tale, let it be a part of it.

I eventually quit running during the pandemic when everything shut down. I had no other option, not because I wanted to.

This is My New Foundation

Everything slowed down. My diversions vanished. My armor broke.

At that point, the reconstruction process started. Truth was the first thing.

I had to tell myself the truth about the things I had kept hidden, even from myself. When I was not feeling well, I stopped acting like I was. I stopped downplaying my trauma to appease other people. Grief made me stop smiling. And I began to stand tall, speak clearly, and present myself genuinely.

I began to share my tale. Everything. Not just the portions that are proud.

The anguish followed. It is ancient pain, not new. Buried beneath decades of silence, that is. It no longer matters what you tell yourself. However, it does. Because of that agony, you get defensive when someone approaches you too closely, you stay busy, and occasionally, you push away those who are attempting to show you love.

I allowed myself to feel it.

And through that suffering, I found my true strength—not the sort that appears on a résumé or in a uniform, but the kind that comes from persevering, choosing to forgive, and choosing to love yourself despite everything.

This is My New Foundation

I began to love myself—not in the manner the world suggests, but rather how God commands us to: as a unique individual who is nonetheless deserving despite suffering. I gave up looking for approval. I gave up attempting to "prove" anything. And instead of performance, I began to live for serenity.

Love was the only thing that made that serenity possible.

My wife is patient and solid in her affection.

My children are calm and dependable.

My friends' love is long-lasting and well-earned.

And even when I felt unworthy, God's love remained unwavering.

I began to think I was enough all the time and stopped asking if I was.

But faith gave me more stability than anything else. It was faith, not religion that held when all else failed. Not customary. However, a relationship—with God, truth, and purpose.

I do not know everything. Not everything is clear to me.

However, I am aware that my foundation is now faith rather than fear.

It is based on what I have learned, not on what I have lost.

This is My New Foundation

It is also mine.

What I consider myself to be is more important than who accepts me.

It is peaceful at this new foundation. There is no need for applause. There is no requirement for agreement. All that is required is to live it out every day with honesty, modesty, and thankfulness.

I remain a human. I was still in pain. I continue to make errors.

But now I am planted.

Grounded in reality.

Painfully forged.

Love has strengthened it.

Led by faith.

I now live to recognize my development rather than to run away from my history.

I now bear wisdom instead of humiliation.

I also stop asking, "Why me?"

With what I have survived, I ask myself, "What can I do?"

My new foundation is this.

It is not pompous, but it is unbreakable.

CHAPTER 12

A LIFE SHAPED BY TRUTH

Owning My Story, Honoring My Scars

Chapter 12:

A Life Shaped by Truth
Owning My Story, Honoring My Scars

I was a master of appearances for the majority of my life. Even in the face of grief, I could smile. I could crumble in silence and lead with determination. I was living behind a meticulously constructed version of myself, so even if I put in 14-hour workdays, wore the appropriate uniform, and produced results, I would still feel empty when I got home. One that provided comfort to others. One that appeared powerful, well-groomed, and prosperous. But it's a completely honest one.

The truth was too jumbled. Too hurtful. Too uncooked.

In actuality, I had gone through experiences that many children's have been through in their life in memory. I felt ashamed of something that was not mine and that I had developed coping strategies that, although praised in the military, were signs of hidden suffering.

I wore my pain like camouflage, with a contrived sense of control, ambition, and achievement on top of it. However, simply packing things neatly does not alleviate the anguish. It waits. It expands. In the silence, it emerges. Additionally, it robs you of closeness, tranquility, and self-worth until you

This is My New Foundation

eventually no longer recognize yourself when you look in the mirror.

I had to sit by myself when COVID-19 shut down the globe. Not a sound. Avoid being distracted. Only me. The reality started to surface at that point.

And I could either continue to hide or begin to recover. I was mad but I went with healing.

That required me to publicly acknowledge things I would never have otherwise: that I had PTSD but did not want to call it that; that childhood abuse influenced my self-perception, relationships with women, and shame; that my sexual behavior, which I used to think was "just being a man," was a pattern of seeking approval to calm an inner storm; and that my anger was not just anger but grief I had not allowed myself to feel.

Although it was not easy, it was essential to tell the truth because your story will own you unless you take ownership of it.

I took away from the silence that you cannot cure what you refuse to accept. If you are scared to dig, you cannot grow. Additionally, you cannot find serenity by pretending that nothing is wrong.

I, therefore, quit acting.

I began to talk, really talk. To God. To my therapist. To the mirror. To people and friends who would listen. Not all people want to hear your problems, but there a few close friends that share your challenges or have their own challenges to share. I started examining the aspects of myself that I had previously avoided: the wounded child, the abandoned spouse, the betrayed man, and the weary soldier. And I began to embrace them instead of blaming them.

Because, in all honesty, I made the best of what I had. I am also learning how to use what I know more effectively now.

Everything changed as the truth was revealed.

As a result, I no longer present myself in my marriage as someone who must "win" but rather as someone who seeks understanding. It altered my parenting style by requiring me to be emotionally present in addition to supplying. It altered my leadership style by demonstrating vulnerability rather than requiring perfection.

It altered my self-perception. Not as damaged. Not in the role of a victim. Not as a man whose faults define him.

However, as a man who has persevered, changed, and discovered the bravery to be authentic.

Your history does not vanish when you embrace your truth. It implies that your history no longer determines your value.

Because you are no longer carrying the burden of your former self, you can walk lightly. It means that instead of expressing regret about your narrative, you should start celebrating the fortitude required to endure it.

So here I am. Still recovering. I am still learning. Still expanding.

But at last—unrestricted.

Because the truth completes you rather than merely frees you.

CHAPTER 13

THERE'S ONE MORE TRUTH

For most of my career, I designed in silence—most notably, a data-at-rest security solution that has quietly protected the backbone of the U.S. military's digital infrastructure for over 15 years. As of 2025, it's still active, still operational, still defending our nation's most sensitive systems. But it doesn't bear my name.

Chapter 13:

There's One More Truth

I have created in silence for most of my career, most notably a data-at-rest security solution that has silently safeguarded the foundation of the U.S. military's digital infrastructure for over 15 years. As of 2025, it is still operating and active, protecting the most critical systems in our country. But my name is not on it.

It is the unstated price of service.

They tell you in uniform: "The government owns your intellectual property." The message is the same for contractors. The system absorbs the creativity, wisdom, and genius you contribute. Your legacy becomes invisible, and your labor becomes the property of the government. Defense innovators frequently see their ideas rebranded, standardized, and honored under someone else's banner, especially when they lack the support of a Fortune 500 company or the privilege of notoriety, while tech giants like IBM or Microsoft patent and benefit from similar innovations.

To be honest, I was not aware of the FARs, the Federal Acquisition Regulations that govern every aspect of procurement. Nobody gave me a handbook. I discovered them the hard way—through lost chances, omitted clauses, and the

This is My New Foundation

silent understanding that performing a good job is not enough to succeed in this field. It is important to know the regulations that determine who initially receives the job. Although I was not the intended recipient of the FARs, I had to learn them to survive. Every error served as a teaching moment. Every mistake is a valuable lesson learned. I eventually quit playing catch-up and began playing wise.

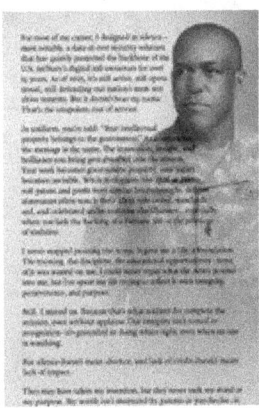

I continued to give the Army praise throughout it all. It provided me with both a foundation and a life. I did not waste the training, the discipline, or the learning opportunities. I have dedicated my life to reflecting the integrity, tenacity, and purpose that the Army instilled in me, even if I could never fully return it.

But I went on. Because warriors accomplish the task, even in the absence of praise. Doing the right thing even when no one is looking is the foundation of our integrity, not accolades.

However, quiet does not imply absence, and a lack of acknowledgment does not imply deficiency.

They may have stolen my idea, but they never stole my purpose or my thoughts. My legacy—the warriors I trained, the systems I created, the doors I opened—measures my value more than patents or salaries. Nobody can steal that kind of wealth.

My inventions did not make me wealthy. However, I developed conviction, clarity, and the guts to tell the truth. I see a visionary when I look in the mirror—a man who sacrificed everything, suffered great losses, yet never lost himself. The goal of resilience is to return with newfound wisdom and the courage to share your story, not just to bounce back.

In both my contracting and military positions, I safeguarded people in addition to managing systems. There was a soldier, a spouse, a child, or a federal employee just trying to go about their daily lives behind every firewall, every encrypted folder, and every authentication process. Protecting personally identifiable information (PII) was always mission-critical.

Federal networks include some of the most sensitive information in the world, including payroll, classified clearance information, Social Security numbers, medical records, and operating plans. Identity theft, blackmail, and espionage are all potential outcomes if this data falls into the wrong hands.

These are facts that I have witnessed come to pass, not just hypotheticals.

My data-at-rest approach was, therefore, about care rather than mere compliance. I created digital armor for those who were unaware of their true vulnerability.

Since the system was not meant to offer a definitive response, nobody had one. I, therefore, created my solution, which utilizes the Common Access Card (CAC) certificate of each user to generate encrypted files in real time that are accessible only by the cardholder. To provide seamless, user-transparent protection, I automated and simplified the Windows Encrypting File System (EFS), which operates quietly in the background.

My approach ensured that encrypted information could be recovered without compromising access or integrity by retrieving and securely storing the original certificate in case a user acquired a new CAC or their PC crashed.

The outcome? An automated, user-transparent encryption architecture that improved security, ensured compliance and offered previously unheard-of operational visibility. A straightforward inquiry turned into a game-changing solution that protected systems for many years.

This is My New Foundation

Not boastfully, but with great responsibility, my task was important. The weight of life was taken into consideration when writing every line of code. Not only was my program intelligent, but it saved lives.

Yes, it was painful to see it rebranded for financial gain and deprived of its original provenance. However, they never accepted my "why." In today's digital world, cybersecurity is essential for survival. And I continued to attend that mission.

I consider myself fortunate to have had answers in my spirit—insights from a higher power rather than from textbooks. After reading a white paper from Microsoft, I had a dream that gave me the idea for my data-at-rest solution. I viewed automation as a smooth, scalable, and secure system that has been safeguarding sensitive military data for over 15 years, in contrast to the paper's description of manual encryption.

That is the way God operates. He infuses what appears to be mundane with revelation. I was never working alone, even when I was silent and uncredited.

My Mind was the tool, but divine guidance was the fuel.

CHAPTER 14
FORGED IN PAIN
WHAT TRIED TO BREAK ME, BUILT ME

Chapter 14:

Forged in Pain; What Tried to Break Me, Built Me

Pain does not request authorization. It is all-consuming, erratic, and unwanted, like a sudden hurricane. It upends everything in its path as it rips through your life. Finally, it passes, leaving you to look at the rubble and question whether you will ever feel complete again.

I used to think that suffering was something to dodge, ignore, neglect, and bury well beneath work, obligation, and responsibility. I learned that survival strategy as a child. You completely lose your sense of security when life does not feel safe. You get harder. You stop talking. It is too risky to glance back, so you keep moving forward like a machine.

However, I have come to realize that we carry what we do not confront. And the more unrecognized anguish we bear, the heavier it becomes until it finally breaks us.

Having experienced childhood trauma, I know with certainty that no child should ever have to endure such pain. I've been shaped by betrayals within my own family — wounds that cut deeper than anything the outside world could inflict. I've served through inefficient procedures and malfunctioning systems that demanded my best while slowly draining my spirit.

This is My New Foundation

I've watched the business I poured myself into many challenges during COVID-19. And I've sat in the stillness of COVID-19, stripped of distractions, forced to face a sadness I had never truly allowed myself to feel.

Every chapter of my life was filled with pain. And I allowed it to define me for a time. However, after that, something changed. I began to question, "What now?" instead of, "Why me?" I started to view pain as a forge—a location where pressure and heat create something more powerful than what was previously there—rather than as a form of punishment.

I started to understand that pain did not just harm me; it also made me more aware of who I was. It made me realize what was important. It dispelled the falsehoods I held about my value. It helped me return to what is true—faith, family, peace, and purpose—and exposed the false gods I had created around status, money, and performance.

I learned via pain to slow down, focus, and hear God's quiet voice rather than the cacophony of the outside world. It showed me that showing vulnerability is a sign of strength, not weakness. That it is smart to seek aid; it is not a sign of weakness. Although it is not a straight line, mending is always possible.

On certain days, I doubted that I would survive. There were days when I began to doubt everything due to the weight of regret, memories, and fatigue. Even so, I continued because of something fire-forged within me.

Since I have endured worse, I have been through more difficult experiences. And each scar on my body and soul serves as evidence that I am still alive.

I become a man who never gives up because of pain. A man who does not have to get out of his uncomfortable chair. A man capable of speaking the truth, even if it is unpleasant. A guy who can carry his scars into the future as reminders of his power rather than as indicators of his failure.

If I have learned anything, it is that life will break you. However, it can also help you grow if you let it.

Not despite the agony but because of it.

Chapter 15:

Strengthened by Love; The Quiet Force That Kept Me Standing

When discussing survival, people frequently use terms like tenacity, resilience, and determination—as if a guy could survive a fire solely by endurance. Indeed, such qualities have enabled me to persevere through some of my most trying moments. But if I am being completely honest, willpower alone would not have gotten me this far.

Love was what kept me together, especially when I felt like I was on the verge of crumbling. Not the ostentatious, theatrical type that displays impressive motions for the world to witness. I am referring to the silent type. The stable, unyielding kind. When the truth becomes muddy, or the strong guy suddenly loses his strength, that love does not falter.

That is the kind of love my wife, Hazel, has shown me. A steady presence during the tempest. We have experienced our fair share of arguments, quiet moments, and periods of separation in the heart. However, love always returned to the center. Not because everything was ideal but rather because we consistently made the difficult decision to choose one another.

I did not feel lovable at times before and during the pandemic. When I emotionally shut down due to depression, PTSD, and irritation. When I was struggling to find the right words to describe my feelings, however, she remained.

In silence, at times. Obstinately at times. But with love, always. In her company, I discovered aspects of myself that I had previously believed had vanished.

My children's affection has also sustained me. Each one contains a fragment of my life's narrative and testimony. One of the greatest blessings of my life has been witnessing them develop, falter, achieve, and then rise again. They motivated me to keep fighting, to stay alive and involved, even though they did not always comprehend what I was going through on the inside.

As fathers, many men go through the motions of fatherhood without ever truly understanding their journey. This is a passage I wrote to share what I believe makes a man — not just in title, but in truth in chapter the Season of a Man.

It's something I wish I had known years ago. Not just for the sake of my own growth, but for the love I could have expressed more fully, the pain I could have named earlier, and the legacy I could have shaped more consciously.

And then there is the love that appeared out of the blue. When I had not phoned for months, friends answered the phone. I had people from my past who came back when I needed them.

This is My New Foundation

Neighbors who made an appearance. Veterans who served as a reminder to me that fraternity endures beyond the uniform. Even though their comments were not always the best, their presence was crucial.

Love finds a way to manifest itself even in tense relationships and broken family dynamics—whether through a gentle remark, a cherished memory, or a tiny act of kindness or forgiveness.

I have also received love from the community. People who understand what it means to show up have surrounded me from Detroit to Charlotte. Whether it was a quiet coffee discussion or a reunion on 8 Mile, those connections helped me put things back together that I was not even aware were off.

Love does not solve every problem. However, it gives you the willpower to continue showing up. When your legs fail, you have something to rely on. It serves as a reminder that you are not alone in life, no matter how challenging it may become.

I have been knocked down more times than I would like to admit, traumatized, and toughened by experience. However, love has also made me entire, steady, and softer.

Love was not always what I had anticipated. It appeared to be a matter of patience at times. Like a difficult conversation sometimes. Like quiet that remained near at times. However, it was present. And I was saved by it.

I now know this to be true as I stand on my new foundation: Love did more than merely support me. It made me stronger.

It helped to ease the agony.

It provided a reason for mending.

It elevated survival to a religious ideal.

I do not take it for granted, either. No more. Because I am aware that I would not be here if it were not for love. Not this guy. Not with this heart. Not with this clarity.

There comes a time when you can no longer get by with strength, experience, and intelligence alone. I have experienced each of those. I have drawn on the grit I developed growing up in Detroit, combined with my business acumen and military discipline. However, none of that was able to calm the pandemic's storms, the memories it uncovered, or the emptiness that persisted after so many losses. Toughness was not what kept me together when all of that failed, and my foundation started to crumble.

The act of faith.

Religion is not a performance. Avoiding the formalities. But unadulterated, intimate faith emerges when you are by yourself in a room, pleading for understanding. The kind of religion that always provides presence but does not always provide answers. Neither a song nor a sermon revealed God to me. In the places where no one else could reach me, in the quiet, under the weight of my questions, I found Him.

I had faith before. I saw visions as a child, times when I felt like I was part of something bigger than myself. I requested baptism at the age of 10 because I felt compelled to do so, not because someone told me to. God was the sole constant in the upheaval of my youth for some reason.

However, my relationship with God became quieter as life happened—marriage, military duty, business, and ambition. Not gone, but hidden away on a shelf, like a book that I didn't have time to open. I was not listening, but I still had faith. I was not looking. Before the pandemic stopped everything, I was too busy creating, surviving, and repairing things and people.

At that point, I resumed my conversations with God. Not in a strict sense. Not flawlessly. Just be honest. I prayed for clarity rather than blessings. For peace, not for triumph. Not for an escape route but for the fortitude to persevere.

God then responded. It was always what I needed, not necessarily what I wanted.

He emphasized that my identity was independent of my financial account, my work title, and the acceptance of others. That I was deserving because I was His, not because of anything I had done. That I could have love without having to seem like I was right. I did not deserve that grace. It was given to me.

I was able to reframe anything with faith. The failures, the trauma, and the losses were not penalties. They were invitations to develop, heal, and submit.

I gained the ability to relinquish control. Should ask, "God, what are You trying to show me through this?" rather than attempting to cure everything. Everything changed when that question was asked. It took me from fear to trust and from rage to awareness.

I am a man with a calling, not merely a man with a history, and I live by intention.

And that calling—to lead with love—is very obvious.

To lead a purposeful life.

To live by faith.

Things started to change as I submitted, not instantly or suddenly, but in a significant way.

I never imagined that I could forgive others.

This is My New Foundation

I pardoned myself.

I gave up attempting to establish my value.

I began to live off of it.

I stopped questioning why I had to go through so much.

I began to inquire about how I could utilize it to help other people.

My faith has evolved into the compass I use every day, not just during emergencies. It influences how I love, how I make decisions, and how peaceful I am. It serves as the cornerstone of my new, unbreakable existence.

I still struggle with skepticism and meet obstacles. I am aware today, though, that I am not alone. I have got my steps straight. I have a purpose in life. Additionally, my suffering adds to a greater narrative that God is still crafting.

It was not always simple with faith.

However, it enabled everything.

I have stopped relying on instinct to guide me through life.

CHAPTER 16
RECLAIMING LIFE DURING COVID ON THE RIVER

We caught something better.
We caught stillness in a world
that had lost its rhythm.

BILL BAILEY

Chapter 16:

Reclaiming Life During COVID-19 on the River

My brother Money and I understood we needed space—not just physical isolation, but emotional, mental, and spiritual release—during the height of COVID-19 when terror and uncertainty gripped the world. After my flight to Detroit, we drove north for five hours in search of salmon, which we were unaware we were searching for.

Salmon, indeed.

We never thought Michigan would have places like these—untamed rivers, whispering woodlands, and trout strong enough to swim upstream as if born to defy the odds—when we were growing up in Detroit, filled with concrete and exhaust. We had the impression that we had wandered into a secret area of the state that they had neglected to show us when we were children.

When we accepted my friend Tony's sister's invitation to go fishing, they treated us like family. They were familiar with the terrain, the cadence of the water, and the silent endurance needed. Coffee in hand, we piled into the truck and drove through the chilly breath of dawn every morning, long before the sun even rose. Silently, the river welcomed us—not the heavy sort, but the type that seeps into your bones and starts to mend things.

While the majority of the group stayed in campers, Money and I discovered a modest hotel full of blue-collar men who were also fishers; many of them had weathered faces and were early risers. These were the ones who found a church standing motionless and casting a line, not in pews. There was a peaceful connection founded on a mutual love of nature, water, and the pursuit of truth.

We ate dinner on the shores of Lake Michigan one evening after a hard day on the river. Without thinking, I exclaimed, "This looks like Hawaii," as the sun sank into the lake, transforming the sky into a fiery blaze. That was the extent of its beauty. That something so magnificent had been waiting here—in our backyard—all along astounded me.

At that point, a more profound reality became apparent.

We hardly ever left our neighborhood as kids in Detroit. The police stopped us each time we passed 8 Mile Road. Being mobile and Black was already a red flag. Road excursions seemed more like hazards than adventures. Our mother kept us near because the outer world did not always feel safe, not because we were not curious.

This is My New Foundation

Therefore, nobody informed us of this version of Michigan—not in this way, not as something we could claim or touch.

Reclaiming space was the main goal of this excursion, not only catching salmon. Every cast, each clear breath of air, and each peaceful mile served as a reminder that we, too, belong here.

I also learned something surprising from the river.

Fishermen support one another.

It made no difference where you were from or who you were. Someone, whether Black, White, Latino or not, would come over with their net and assist you in landing the salmon if you hooked it and began wrestling it. No inquiries. Without hesitation.

There was an unsaid kinship, a silent understanding. To get a man's assistance, you did not have to know his name. All you needed to do was immerse yourself in the moment, respect the river, and be fully present. Everyone watched out for one another in those currents. It has nothing to do with politics or race. It had to do with being human.

And I got it because things do not always operate that way in the world back home.

However, we were merely fishermen on that river. Only people. And the world felt wonderful, right, and easy for a few holy hours every day.

The ride was restorative, too. Long highways, background music that is not too loud, and silence that gives way to talk. We discussed our mother for the first time in years.

We chuckled about our differences and how she loved us in different ways.

Her favorite thing was my brother Money. Everyone was aware of it. He possessed her kindness, humor, and warmth. His jokes would make her laugh as if they were the first time she had ever heard happiness. They spoke quietly, each with their cadence. I simply played a different part, so I was not envious.

It was me who did it. The one who fixes things. The son of "Doobie." I was the one who called if there was a problem. Same mom. The same affection. Distinct connections. Distinct sons.

And at some point along that drive, we realized that more profoundly than before. No bitterness, only insight. Just tranquility.

That weekend, we did not catch any salmon. But my friend Tony sister husband gave us two. We did, however, catch something better.

In a world that had lost its beat, we managed to capture silence. A moment of absolute beauty that, until we were in the center of it, seemed to belong to someone else. We witnessed

This is My New Foundation

perspective, laughter, and the subdued reminder that healing can occasionally appear beside the person who has known your story from the beginning, standing in a chilly river and wearing waders.

It was more than just a vacation. It was more than just a fishing excursion. It was a welcome home.

Reflection Verse for the reader:

"He leads me beside still waters. He restores my soul." – Psalm 23:2–3

Devotional Prompt:

Where have you found unexpected healing in a place you never imagined you belonged?

What might God be using in your life right now to restore your soul?

This is My New Foundation

CHAPTER 17
Marion "Money" Browder
The Brother Who Taught Me Grace

Chapter 17:

Marion "Money" Browder – The Brother Who Taught Me Grace

Some ties become lifelines and go beyond blood. That was how I felt about Marion Browder, my brother. I dubbed him "Money" because I was unable to pronounce "Marion" from an early age. To be honest, it fits, and the term remained. For those who loved him, Money was more than just a term; it was a power, a presence, and a rhythm.

In addition to being my brother, Money was also my best friend, my sounding board, my mirror, and frequently my moral compass. He was the only one who could both criticize me and encourage me. "Dennis, it is not what you say—it is how you say it," he was the first to advise me. That counsel has served as a constant reminder to me throughout my life to lead with presence and intention as much as words. He showed me how to present difficult realities in a gentle manner.

Money was tall, and charismatic 6'5" when he enter high school as a student. He refused to join the team despite the football coach's entreaties, stating that he did not want to harm anyone. He was just that—a kind giant with a warrior's heart. He led with kindness at all times, yet he was not scared of conflict.

It was too early for Money. He came up with the name "Power House" at the age of 13, which perfectly encapsulated his attitude and personality. Legends like Ric Flair were among the wrestlers he later trained at Detroit's Power House Gym. He worked there for ten years, continuously providing for our family. He brought pizza and wings home from Premo's Pizza every Saturday. He frequently loaned us his automobile and paid my bills without asking. He handed me a pair of Doctor J breakaway pants and Nike leather shoes in 1978, and I will always remember that day. That gesture still holds great significance for me now.

Money once met President George H.W. Bush while working as a cook at West Point in the 1980s. Traveling to destinations like the Kentucky Derby, San Francisco, Tampa, Palm Beach, Georgia, the Carolinas, and even Colorado was something he treasured. He welcomed every location and every second.

But Money's path was not without suffering. Benzedrine, a stimulant that was originally used to treat children's hyperactivity, was prescribed to him as a child. I was the quiet one who never took medicine and only spoke when spoken to. However, Money, who was full of life and energy, received something that would affect him for the rest of his days. Because it was addictive, Benzedrine became a nuisance for him. The harm had already been done, even though the drug's terrible effects led to the U.S. government eventually banning it.

Money constantly supported me despite his difficulties. I would listen to him if he pulled me aside and told me, "You are wrong." It was based on love rather than condemnation. He gave me clarity when I was unsure. He reminded me to be empathetic when I was being too severe. He made me chuckle when I needed it.

People never forget the kind of man he was. Money could brighten any space with his long, curly hair, radiant grin, and easy ability to connect.

Then he departed on March 2, 2023.

It was a rupture, not simply a date. After the COVID-19 pandemic, the world was finally gathering its breath, but I had lost mine. His leaving left a gap that was more profound than any grief I had ever experienced. This was the most difficult battle for me to survive out of all of them.

He abruptly, brutally, and unexpectedly passed away after a heart attack. I fell into severe despair after the loss. Nothing had prepared me for the stillness following Money's death, even though I had experienced military service, betrayal, failure, death, and even pandemic isolation. My life's soundtrack had just ceased.

He was sixty years old. Too young. Too colorful. I still hear his voice, and I carry his teachings close to my heart. His favorite quote, "It is not what you say—it is how you say it," makes me smile.

A Story I Never Thought

In March 2025, I thought about my brother, who had influenced my worldview and was also my closest confidant. I will admit that I never believed the majority of the crazy stories he used to tell me since they always seemed too fantastical. One of the most bizarre was that he used to collect Money for the Mob when he was twenty years old. I always assumed that was just Money being Money, making up stories to dazzle or amuse people.

I was also getting my roof redone at this time. To my surprise, the man who came to check it out turned out to be the Italian professional wrestler, Gary Sabaugh. He seemed strangely familiar. I could not help but ask him whether he knew someone named Money as we were talking. He gave a negative response. But when I mentioned Byrum, his reaction was unexpected.

"Tony?" he inquired.

Indeed, that is my brother, I said.

His next statement, "My brother and I used to collect for the Mob," came as a shock to me.

I was blown away. For years, I believed my brother's stories to be pure fiction. And here was someone corroborating that he was speaking the truth: a professional wrestler I just so happened to encounter. As I stood there in shock, I understood that Money had always been telling the truth. He then told me stories about my brother and the Power House gym in Detroit, which confirmed other stories my brother Money had previously told me.

Money, you were more than just my brother. You were the balance to my fire, the grace when I needed it, and the truth when I needed it most. Even when you are not physically present, your contagious laughter, your unfailing love, and your deep wisdom still serve as my compass.

This life—this chapter—is for you.

CHAPTER 18

A Son Who Loved His Mom with Respect— By Any Means

Chapter 18:

A Son Who Loved His Mom with Respect—By Any Means

In a world that did not protect innocence, my mother's friends took on the role of protectors. I gained survival skills under their guidance, such as how to carry myself with my belongings, read a room before entering, and listen quietly. There was no other option except to grow up quickly.

At one point, Auntie Minnie asked to adopt me. Maybe she could sense my dislocation and realize how much I needed. However, my mother declined—for I was her son, even though we were emotionally apart. And I stayed faithful.

Naturally, I took over as her caregiver for the last thirteen years of her life as her health worsened. I honored her because it was right, not because our past was flawless. I pointed out what was lacking. Rather, I offered peace and respect.

I asked her the question that had been ringing in my ears for decades: "Mom, why did you put so much pressure on me when I was a kid?" throughout her final two years. She replied with a soft smile, "Because I knew you could handle it." All I wanted to hear were those straightforward words.

It was a compliment in her way, the type that only a mother can offer without using words.

This is My New Foundation

I continued to provide for her financially in 2005 as her needs grew—no questions asked. However, one day, I changed my strategy and said, "Mom, I will pay your bills directly instead of sending money." Silently, she nodded. I questioned her later when she attempted to give me her house notes. "How is there a note when this house is paid off?" She had taken out a home equity line of credit, her bent head and quiet tone making it clear.

My nephew then called. "You must come get your mother, Dennis." She is having difficulties, and her home is not as tidy as it used to be. I took off right away. I could tell by one glance that it was time. To make sure she would be comfortable on her first journey, I purchased her a first-class ticket in seat 1A. She begged to drive, but I told her that winter mountain roads in Virginia and West Virginia were too dangerous for her. Only twice would my mother take a plane: once to travel to me in the South and again to Detroit for her everlasting rest.

Since our bedrooms were all upstairs, she was unable to reside with us due to her mobility concerns. But I would not allow her to suffer or lose her honor. I located her in a quiet one-story apartment only two miles from my house. No steps. Do not worry. I made sure she was safe—because sons do that.

The call that shook me then came.

"William?" the man inquired.

170

This is My New Foundation

"My name is not William," I firmly stated. "It is Mr. Bailey."

He continued using "William" as though my correction had no effect.

He introduced himself as a Chase Bank agent and stated that they were preparing to take back my mother's house. She had obtained a home equity loan for $44,000. I had a gut feeling that things were not quite right. My mom was not a driver. She would not have been the only one to make such a financial choice. That bank was where someone had brought her. She had been led into murky waters by someone.

It is still unclear what happened to the $44,000. My mother remained silent when I tried to bring it up. Her eyes, those eyes that could say "That is enough" without making a sound, would halt the conversation before it even started.

Her eyes had always said more than words could express. I read about suffering, arrogance, obstinacy, and survival. I had learned to read these unspoken messages like holy scripture since I was her son. Her unspoken language made perfect sense to me.

I told him bluntly, "I will see you in court,".

After I engaged a lawyer, the truth came out fast. It was a mistake to approve the loan because it consumed more than 70% of her fixed income. Blatantly exploitative lending. In a letter to the court, my lawyer exposed my mother's trickery and explained how her son, a North Carolina U.S. Army serviceman, had intervened to recover what was legally hers.

The judge looked directly at the Chase Bank lawyer. "I strongly suggest you make a deal with Mr. Bailey—because you are not going to like what I do next."

The bank man called again the next day. His tone was different this time.

"Mr. Bailey."

We could now understand one another.

I informed him that the $44,000 was no longer there. "I did not see a dime, but I am not sure where it went. You will get $22,000 from me. I secretly feared my mother had given away the funds to family. It felt reasonable to split the blame—I carried my guilt for not keeping a closer eye on her activities, and the bank was responsible for authorizing an unsuitable loan. We both acknowledged our roles in the circumstances as a result of this compromise.

He accepted without question. Negotiation is not required. It was resolved.

In addition to saving a house, I had also saved her honor by defending her property when she was unable to do so for the

This is My New Foundation

simple reason that she was my mother, not for praise or recognition. Additionally, I was her son.

She lost her mobility due to the virus two months after she moved to Charlotte. I made arrangements for her to live in an assisted living facility in a private room. Although I was in Augusta, Georgia, for business, I would travel up to Charlotte every weekend to spend Saturdays with my family.

She felt the love of our family. We kept her clothes clean, took care of her, and were always there for her. The regular company of my granddaughter and stepson made her days more cheerful. She thrived on human interaction, so I took her to our house for every family get-together.

We went to dinner or the beach when her strength permitted. Since red is her favorite color, I made sure her outfits were always in style. For her, strength and beauty went hand in hand. I wanted her always to feel beautiful.

The protection, sacrifice, and presence of a mother and son demonstrate their love in inexpressible ways. Although the Bible instructs us to respect our parents, this respect extends beyond the text. It is ingrained in a son's heart to become his mother's guardian, safeguarding her welfare out of love rather than just obligation.

And I did precisely that.

This is My New Foundation

The underlying premise of my new foundation is a profound truth: children are not only here to support their parents but also to eventually honor, uplift, and enrich their lives in return.

Through their example and teachings, our parents impart valuable lessons to us. As we grow up, we give back by being patient, loving, listening, paying attention to advice, and becoming self-sufficient. Such love relieves their anxieties, eases their loads, and demonstrates the success of their sacrifices.

We give them back by being present, taking action, and having a purpose.

My new foundation is that.

Red was my mother's favorite color. She loved beauty—bright hues, sophisticated fashion. She appropriately earned two life celebrations: one in Detroit, Michigan, and one in Charlotte, North Carolina. To honor her, the cities that influenced our journey came together in tribute.

As Money put it, "Mom always thought of herself as a queen—and she went out like a queen."

As she deserved, she left with honor; my brother was surrounded by affection.

I do not feel guilty or regret anything. From the world she knew, my mother provided me with the finest existence possible. "I may not be the best mother in the world—but you kids always knew where I was," she said, and her words still reverberate today. I was at home.

She was, too. Always.

Memories flooded my mind with shocking urgency during the COVID-19 pandemic. Depression began to set in. From its hiding place, PTSD came out. I had been silently, consistently, and uncomplainingly carrying the burden of trauma for decades. COVID-19, however, broke that cautious silence.

It entered my spirit, dreams, and memory. My head turned into a battlefield, with explosions everywhere. Not a warning. No way out. Everything came crashing in at once. The quiet around them was not quiet; it thundered. Every moment of seclusion just made its rage louder.

My existence continued to replicate itself in that silence. Every suppressed emotion and whispered hurt sprang to the surface. The strain. The suffering. The weight of things I had never unpacked but had carried. It all came back as a destructive deluge rather than a peaceful tide.

Not only did COVID-19 shut out the world, but it also tore down my inner walls and opened up every part of me that had been sealed.

This is My New Foundation

I discovered the reality at that point: we were never intended to live alone. Our purpose is to connect—to talk, to laugh, to be present. Still, there I was, ensnared in my thoughts, encircled by specters and unbound recollections. Emotionally imprisoned, not just physically separated.

And loneliness like that does not whisper.

It yells.

Even to the most powerful man.

My New Foundation Is This

For the majority of my life, I thought that silence was a sign of strength. I should carry it if I can. True men persevered rather than broke. I believed that this belief would shield me, so I wore it like armor. However, quiet turns into a jail of its own. Pain only wears you out; it does not make you stronger.

Everything fell apart when COVID-19 shut down the globe, including my routine, rhythm, and business. And I did, at last. No longer the man with answers, the leader, or the supplier. Simply put, it's broken.

The truth is, however, that God works greatest when you break things.

I found a new strength in that silence, one of surrender rather than perseverance. I learned to pray more than to plan and to listen more than to talk. I gave up trying to save myself for the first time in years. I started to recover.

Through layers of treatment, faith, introspection, and honest talks with God, the healing came gradually. I re-established my connection with His provided dreams, those predawn visions that provided answers, and that heavenly voice that pushed me ahead when reason told me to back off.

As I looked at my scattered parts, I realized that this was an internal reconstruction rather than a loss.

Chapter 19:

This Is My New Foundation

This is an invitation for everybody who has ever felt uncertain, shattered, forgotten, or silenced. You are not by yourself. You are still redeemable.

It is not too late to start over. Not even close. No matter how long you have been carrying your burdens, how many times life has struck you down, or how far you have wandered, it does not matter. There is yet time. Maintain your grace. There is still more to do.

Start with the truth—the unvarnished kind that speaks from the heart and removes performance. Instead of avoiding discomfort, walk through it. Please give it a name. Feel it. Do not let it define you; instead, let it teach you. Hold on to love—the sort that reminds you that being alone was never the goal and loves your times of unworthiness. Give yourself over to faith—not because you have the answers, but because you believe that God does.

My new foundation is this. It is based on surrender rather than achievement or perfection. Formed by accepting my story rather than running away from it, uncovering hidden strengths, and learning from unpleasant lessons. It stands sturdy, honest, and healed while resting on the fissures that almost broke me.

This is My New Foundation

Grace, faith, forgiveness, and the everyday decision to resist the urge to give up are what bind it. Have hope if you are standing amid the debris of what used to be everything. You can recover from pain, shame, and loss just as easily as I can. Your suffering is not the end of your tale. Your past does not define you.

Even though the basis has changed, it can yet rise again, stronger, smarter, and more firmly grounded than before. Now is your time to start again, decide to heal, and live a purposeful life. Must remove the disguise and accept your actual self's blueprint.

This is the new foundation I have chosen, not made of stone or brick. Some hurt. Some redeeming. Everything is required. I stopped fleeing, I stopped acting, and I decided to heal; therefore, it stands. Let it serve as a reminder that even after the storm, even after the quiet, and even when it seems impossible to put everything back together, there is always hope for regeneration.

No matter what happens to you, you are not. In the aftermath, you are who you decide to be. Thus, construct faithfully, honestly, and slowly. Allow grace to bridge the gaps. Let your blueprint be guided by purpose. Additionally, keep in mind that the foundation you lay today can one day be the hope of another.

This is My New Foundation

Epilogue: This Is My New Foundation
A Life Built on Truth, Forged in Pain, Strengthened by Love, and Guided by Faith

I fully comprehend the path I have traveled as I stand here now, not as a soldier, a CEO, or even a survivor, but just as a man. More importantly, I now have a better understanding of who I am. Titles, responsibilities, and expectations molded my life's purpose for years. I was a young man attempting to make sense of suffering, a soldier shielding people from my wounds, and an entrepreneur pursuing a legacy—often without sleep. However, none of those things could complete me on their own.

Every journey, including this one, has a point at which survival is no longer the main objective. Getting through is no longer sufficient. Wholeness becomes the objective. Calm. Meaning. And this is where I have come to—not struggling to establish myself, not working hard to get attention, but standing firmly on solid footing and at last announcing: this is my new foundation.

Even though I have had money, it is not the foundation. Although I acquired every stripe, I was not on rank. And not on applause, as I have learned the difference between true visibility and celebration. My new foundation was constructed from the ground up, with layers of truth, forgiveness, and grace.

I wore masks that were praised for years: the provider, the leader, the soldier. The man who had it all figured out was just a man—not Black, White, or Latino. A guy molded by expectations, experience, and survival. I was still bearing the burden of what I had been through, though, despite those masks. Haunted by suffering I had never completely dealt with. Attempting to love myself despite still bleeding wounds I had not yet recognized.

I shut down when COVID-19 shut down the globe. The sound ceased. Distractions vanished. And everything I had buried came to the surface in the silence. Instead of yelling, it whispered clearly: 'It is time.'

The days of hiding behind service were over. It is time to cease healing and begin the difficult but sacred task of wholeness. It was time to stop requesting permission to take a break, cry, and reflect. I had to look at every chapter of my story, even the ones I wanted to tear out and tell myself, "You happened." However, you no longer own me.

Because I now understand that while our past may have shaped who we are, it does not define us. Even if trauma affects us, it does not have the last say. Beyond what we have experienced,

This is My New Foundation

we are more than that. What we decide to do with it defines who we are.

And I have decided to construct. Even if my voice trembles, I have decided to speak my truth. To love despite being disappointed. To forgive—because I do, not because they deserve it. I have decided to pass on my knowledge, not my scars, to my grandchildren. I have decided to live a life that honors God by being both obedient and successful.

I had no choice but to look inward only after everything around me collapsed. The pandemic's silence resonated not only through deserted streets but also deep within me. I had to stop because of that. Should keep this in mind. To consider. And to rebuild after that.

We are not going back to the past. This reconstruction is entirely new. A truth-based life—no more denying what wounded me, no more sugarcoating the past to appease others. I now possess my entire story. Acting as though nothing occurred does not shield you. It merely delays your recovery. My freedom is truth.

Pain is also what molded this life. For decades, I have held trauma in my body, blood, and silence. However, suffering is not the enemy. It was that fire that put me to the test and molded me. More powerful. Smarter. More conscious of my values. I no longer dread pain. It made me, which is why I appreciate it.

Love is what makes this life stronger. It is the sort that endures, not the kind that comes and goes. The calling sort. That is forgiving. When you eventually reveal the truth, that does not bat an eye. I have experienced that type of love—from my spouse, kids, some friends, and even strangers who recognized a quality in me that I had not yet recognized in myself. Love did not come to my aid. It served as a reminder that I was valuable.

And faith is the compass of this life. Anchored faith—the type that endures when everything else fails—is preferable to blind faith. The kind that reminds you that the summit is still in sight as you walk down the valley with them. I found my faith amid the storm, not lost it. I now use it as a compass to guide me through all of my decisions, relationships, and thoughts. Faith restored my voice and gave my narrative purpose.

So here I am. Not the person I was before. I am not exactly who I will be. Yet solidly established on a basis that I can at last rely on.

This is an invitation for everybody who has ever felt uncertain, shattered, forgotten, or silenced. You are not by yourself. You are still redeemable.

This is My New Foundation

It is not too late to start over. Not even close. No matter how long you have been bearing the burden, how many times life has knocked you down, or how far you have strayed from your path, it does not matter. There is yet time. Grace is still present. The future is not yet over.

Start with the truth—the kind that speaks directly from the heart and eliminates performance. Instead of avoiding the pain, walk through it. Please give it a name. Feel it. Do not let it define you; instead, let it teach you. Hold on to love and family—the sort that tells you that you were never meant to do this alone and that welcomes you even when you feel unworthy. Let faith be your compass—not because you know everything, but because you believe that God knows.

My new foundation is this. Success was not the foundation of it. Perfection was not its foundation. The foundation of it was surrender. It developed as a result of me taking ownership of my experience rather than avoiding it, learning from lessons I never requested, and uncovering inner power I never realized existed. It stands sturdy, honest, and healed while resting on the fissures that almost broke me.

Grace, faith, forgiveness, and the daily decision to keep going when everything inside of me wanted to give up are what keep things together.

Therefore, have hope if you are standing amid the debris of what previously meant everything. You can recover from pain, shame, and loss just as easily as I can. Your tale does not end with your suffering. Your past does not define you.

Even though the foundation may have shifted, it can be rebuilt with greater strength, wisdom, and stability. Now is your time to start again, decide to heal, and live a purposeful life. Must remove the disguise and retrieve the blueprint of your true self.

This is the basis I have chosen for myself, not formed of stone or brick. Some hurt. Some redeeming. Everything is required. I stopped fleeing, I stopped acting, and I decided to heal; therefore, it stands. Let it serve as a reminder that even after the storm, even after the silence, and even when it seems impossible to put the pieces back together, a fresh start is always possible.

What occurred to you is not who you are. In the aftermath, you are who you choose to be. Thus, construct faithfully, honestly, and slowly. Allow grace to bridge the gaps. Make purpose your guide. And keep in mind that the foundation you lay today can become the same hope that someone else relies on tomorrow.

Final Chapter: To You, the Reader

My childhood loneliness is one of the many losses I bear. The heartbreak of losing more than fifty friends in the process. and the loss of my brother, Money, who was my best friend and dependable companion. The demise of companies in which I had previously invested my life. Additionally, I had to endure three and a half years of living under the COVID-19 shadow, with my mind racing and the world coming to a standstill.

Certain types of development only become apparent after the storm has gone. Initially, all that is visible are the shattered fragments—the voids, the missed hugs, the questions that never seemed to have solutions. You bear the burden of wasted time and incomplete experiences. You start to realize that something more powerful is going on underneath it all, though, if you dare to examine more closely and take a deep breath through the hollow spots.

Deep roots were penetrating the invisible earth. In the dark, fruits were silently forming.

I can now clearly see them as the longest night comes to an end: love, patience, joy, and faith—all of them flourishing where fear formerly held sway.

I did not say anything to my in-laws for three years because I thought that if I didn't say anything, they wouldn't hear it against me. Nevertheless, rumors continued to spread, occupying the voids left by my silence. When you do not express your anxieties, people fill the void by creating their facts and reshaping reality to fit their needs. When you do not speak, they take control of their imagination.

However, stillness also taught me that the results of adversity subtly manifest themselves in the quiet that follows a storm.

When everything else vanished, including the steady voice at the end of a phone line, the handwritten letter traveling silent miles, and the food left on a doorstep with no expectation of return, love became the linchpin.

The brittle yet intense joy blossomed in unexpected places, such as the warmth of a sunrise, laughter that endured through tears, and the unyielding hope sewn into each little day.

Peace did not arrive because the world became calmer. It arrived because I chose to trust even when the skies remained bleak, trusting that storms are not the conclusion of the story.

Patience evolved into a modest type of courage: learning to live in suspended time without giving up hope.

During those days, I realized that Blaise Pascal's quote rings true: "All of humanity's problems stem from man's inability to sit quietly in a room alone."

His comments resonated deeply within me, reminding me that many of life's most important battles are fought in silence, where endurance, trust, and faith are forged.

In the voids between us, kindness became more audible. In the personal, invisible decisions that molded the unseen fabric of our lives, goodness took root. Not because the path was simple, but because the journey was important, faithfulness hummed its steady melody.

The harsh edges of anxiety and anguish were softened by gentleness. Understanding took the place of the bitterness that attempted to establish itself. Self-control developed into the silent, unseen power that favored compassion over rage, thankfulness over hopelessness, and light over darkness.

Every decision we made turned into a planting, a watering, and a faith that something invisible would endure through our darkest days.

What emerged from the shadows was not merely survival but the start of something holy.

But there are always scars associated with growth. My heart might have become hardened at times by the weight of everything—the betrayals, the loneliness, and the broken promises.

Like so many others, there were times when I went out for emotional support and found nothing but hollowness. The world frequently provides passion instead of love. Selfishness, not safety. Hunger, not honor. It takes more than it offers, despite the claims that it is love. Only faith, time, and truth can mend the wounds it leaves.

It would have been simple for me to get resentful of that. to construct barriers so dense that light would never pass through.

However, I made a different decision.

I have decided that it is still worthwhile to wait for true love—the kind that nurtures, honors, and protects. I decided to think that something genuine still existed, even in a world full of fakes. I decided to have faith in the sacred.

Broken promises and borrowed resentment would not be the cornerstones of my new foundation. It would be based on the silent power I discovered within myself—and the invisible benefits that blossomed when no one else was there.

These fruits are not prizes to show off or medals to wear. They are living examples of the deeper work that has been going on all along; they are silent marvels.

They serve as a reminder that something better—something enduring—was establishing itself even when everything else

This is My New Foundation

seemed to be falling apart. My old world has changed irrevocably. However, what emerged from the darkness—bravery, a more profound love, and patient hope—remains woven into the very fabric of my current identity.

Before the longest night fell, we were different.

We are more powerful. We are more tender. We have gained wisdom.

And we do not go forth empty-handed, bearing these invisible gifts that come from adversity.

> We emerge from the darkness.
>
> We enter the light.

I can now say that as I have gotten to know myself better—who Bill Bailey is—and as my connection with God has grown, life has started to blossom in ways I never could have predicted.

My marriage is going well. My spirit is at peace.

God is wonderful. He guided me through my mental, physical, and spiritual struggles not to destroy me but to demonstrate the straightforward idea that, even when storms rage, a story never ends. Light always prevails at the end of the storm.

Seasons of a Man

There is no single moment when a man becomes who he truly is. He arrives in pieces—through ages, through ache, through revelation. The man at 18 is not the same as the one at 54. At 70, the man is no longer chasing the world but embracing his place within it.

Let me walk you through the seasons.

Age 18; Fire and Firsts

At eighteen, a man burns with possibility. He doesn't yet know how the world works, and he doesn't care—because in his heart, he believes he'll bend it to his will.

He lives loud. Fast. Reckless, perhaps. But real.

Every experience is a first—first love, first heartbreak, first time being truly seen... or dismissed.

He tries on identities like jackets, uncertain which fits. The boy in him lingers, but the man is knocking.

He feels ten feet tall, even as doubt waits quietly in the shadows.

Age 25; Becoming and Belonging

By twenty-five, he begins to build.

He trades some of his fire for focus. The world pushes back now. Dreams are not given they are fought for.

He learns that talent opens doors, but discipline keeps them from closing. He wants to belong—somewhere, with someone, to something.

He may be broken, tired, and stretched thin, but he holds tight to belief.

A belief that he's going somewhere, that his struggle has meaning.

He's no longer asking, "What do I want?"—

He's beginning to ask, "Who am I becoming?"

Age 35; The Weight of Middle Ground

At thirty-five, a man stands in the middle.

He is no longer guessing. He is doing.

He wears many roles now—provider, protector, partner, perhaps father.

Time moves faster, and so does pressure. Every decision carries echoes.

He begins to measure himself not by the potential but by the outcome.

He may wonder silently: "Am I enough?"

He rarely says it out loud, but it lives under his breath.

And still, he presses forward—not for applause, but for peace.

At 35, a man starts to understand **success isn't about standing tall—it's about standing firm.**

Age 54; Reflections and Reckonings

Fifty-four is not the end. It is inventory.

The mirror shows him more than age—it shows legacy.

He begins to reflect not just on what he's built but also on what he's missed.

He revisits the past, not to rewrite it, but to understand it.

Regret has become quieter. Gratitude speaks louder.

He knows now that peace is earned—not through perfection, but through presence.

He asks questions with deeper roots:

"Have I loved well?"

"Will they remember me for who I was or just what I did?"

This is the beginning of becoming an elder—

Not in age alone but in wisdom.

Age 70 — Stillness and Story

At seventy, a man no longer runs. He walks.

He walks through memories, through moments, through meaning.

The world moves quickly around him, but inside—he has found a sacred stillness.

He no longer counts his value in tasks but in truth.

His voice may be softer, but when he speaks—he speaks legacy.

He watches his children—perhaps his grandchildren—carve their paths, and he blesses their journeys, knowing each must find their way.

The man at seventy understands what the man at eighteen could not:

Life is not about conquering the world; it's about living it. It's about becoming whole.

"I lived. I lost. I loved. I mattered."

—The quiet anthem of a life fully lived.

Lessons Learned

Lessons Learned — Introduction

In the military, we call them Lessons Learned and After-Action Reports-a disciplined review of what happened, what went right, what went wrong, and most importantly, what must be learned from it.

This book is no different.

Each chapter you read is its own mission. Some were hard-fought victories. Others were quiet battles of survival. But all of them left something behind-something I had to process, pray through, and carry forward. That's what these Lessons Learned are. Not just a summary-but a spiritual briefing. A reflection. A checkpoint on the road of healing.

I didn't write them to sound wise. I wrote them so you don't feel alone.

These aren't just reflections on my past. They're here to help you walk through your own battles-with clarity, with faith, and with strength. Let them serve as guideposts as you navigate your own terrain.

Not rules-just road signs. Not answers-just reminders.

You are not alone in the forest.

Read on. Reflect. And carry what serves you forward.

Lessons Learned — Chapter 1: The Roots Beneath the Stone
Survival, Secrets, and the Making of a Man

1. **Survival starts early—and it isn't a choice.**

When the world offers no protection, a child quickly learns to read danger, adapt, and survive.

2. **Silence becomes a shield.**

When emotions are unwelcome or unsafe, you learn to suppress your voice-until silence becomes your default.

3. **Pleasing people becomes a survival tool.**

Love gets tangled with performance. You begin to believe that if you're useful, agreeable, or invisible, maybe you'll be safe.

4. **Abandonment leaves invisible scars.**

Even if no one sees the wound, the soul remembers who left, who didn't come back, and who didn't choose you.

5. **Hyper-awareness becomes a lifestyle.**

When you've lived in uncertainty, you read faces, tones, and doors before they open. Survival makes you alert—but also exhausted.

6. **Being the strong one comes at a cost.**

You get labeled as mature, responsible, or brave. But inside, you're carrying weight no child should have to bear.

7. **Your foundation may be cracked—but it still holds.**

The very experiences that hurt you can also form the bedrock of resilience, awareness, and wisdom—if you're willing to look underneath the pain.

8. **Pain doesn't define your future—what truly matters is how you choose to respond to it.**

Growth begins with open dialogue and intentional decisions.

Lessons Learned — Chapter 2: The Power of Presence

From Hardy — my brother, my protector, my example — I learned more in silence than I ever did in sermons. These are the lessons he left without writing them down. Lessons I now live by.

1. **Presence outweighs performance.**

You don't need to speak loudly to make an impact. Being present, fully and consistently, is the loudest love language.

2. **Real strength is quiet.**

Hardy never had to show off. His strength came from being steady, not shouting. From protecting, not posturing.

3. **Actions speak louder than apologies.**

He didn't always say "I love you," but he showed it-in protection, sacrifice, and staying close when things got hard.

4. **Being feared and being loved aren't opposites.**

People respected Hardy because he lived with honor. His loyalty made others feel safe, even when his silence made them nervous.

5. **The strongest feel the most but show the least.**

Just because someone doesn't speak about their pain doesn't mean they aren't carrying it. Hardy taught me how to read pain behind stoicism.

6. **Calm is a form of leadership.**

When life gets loud, people look to the quiet one who doesn't flinch. That was Hardy. That's who I strive to be.

7. **Legacy lives in the shadows.**

You don't have to be the center of attention to leave a lasting mark. Hardy's legacy lives through how I show up for others- steady, strong, and present.

Lessons Learned — Chapter 3: Beyond the Uniform

My military career gave me rank, routine, and responsibility-but it also gave me emotional baggage no uniform could conceal. These are the hard-earned truths I carried home with me.

1. **The uniform gives you identity-but it can take your voice.**

I was trained to obey, not to feel. To push forward, not to process. That silence followed me long after I left the battlefield.

2. **Discipline is powerful-but not if it masks your wounds.**

Structure helped me survive. But healing required unlearning some of what that structure taught me-especially the idea that vulnerability is weakness.

3. **Serving others is noble-but losing yourself isn't.**

I gave everything to the mission. But I didn't realize I had left parts of myself behind. Being useful is good. Being whole is better.

4. **Loyalty can be sacred-or self-sacrificing.**

I stayed in toxic spaces because I confused loyalty with obligation. I had to learn that it's okay to walk away from places that no longer serve your peace.

5. The hardest mission isn't war-it's coming home.

Learning how to live without the uniform was harder than any operation. No roadmap. No orders. Just emotions I'd never been trained to handle.

6. You can't heal on autopilot.

The military taught me to act fast. But healing forced me to slow down, listen, and face what I'd buried under years of "I'm fine."

7. You're more than your rank.

Stripped of the uniform, I had to find out who I really was. That discovery wasn't easy-but it was worth it.

Lessons Learned — Chapter 4: The Value of Mentorship

In the military, I didn't just learn from manuals-I learned from men. Some hard, some kind, some both. Their influence shaped not only the soldier I became but also the man I chose to be when no one was watching.

1. **Leadership is more than giving orders-it's setting a standard.**

The best leaders I served under led by example, not just authority. They didn't just talk about values-they lived them.

2. **A mentor doesn't need to be perfect-they need to be present.**

Some of the greatest lessons came from men who were still figuring things out themselves. Their honesty made them powerful.

3. **Correction without compassion creates fear-not growth.**

The ones who helped me grow didn't just point out my flaws. They showed me how to rise above them.

4. **Respect is earned in the small moments.**

It wasn't just about what they said during a briefing. It was how they treated people when no one was watching that made them unforgettable.

5. **Humility is a leadership trait-not a weakness.**

The mentors I admired most admitted when they were wrong. That humility made them human-and worthy of following.

Guidance can save years of pain.

One right word at the right time can change the direction of a life. I still carry those words today.

6. **Mentorship is legacy in motion.**

Everything I pass on now-whether to my grandkids, colleagues, or readers-comes from someone who once poured into me.

Lessons Learned — Chapter 5: When Legacy Meets the Living

That reunion wasn't just an event-it was a homecoming for my spirit. It reminded me that memory isn't a place we visit alone. It's a table we set for the people who helped raise us, shape us, and carry us through.

1. **Your roots will always call you home.**

Time may pass. People may move. But something sacred lives in the soil of where you came from. Never forget it.

2. **Community is medicine.**

Being around people who "knew you when" has a healing effect no therapist can replicate. It reminds you who you've always been underneath it all.

It's never too late to say "thank you."

The people who showed up for you don't always know what they meant to you. Tell them-while they're still here.

3. **Showing up matters more than showing off.**

The power of that reunion wasn't in how we looked-it was in the fact that we came. That we remembered.

4. **Some of the strongest bonds are built in silence.**

This is My New Foundation

We didn't need long speeches or deep conversations. Sometimes a nod, a hug, or a shared laugh says everything that needs to be said.

5. **Honor your past, but don't get stuck in it.**

That day reminded me: we can carry our stories without living inside them. Our past should inform us-not imprison us.

6. **Legacy lives in faces, not just memories.**

Looking around at that reunion, I saw versions of my younger self in every smile. The past wasn't gone-it was alive in all of us.

Lessons Learned — Chapter 6: The Journey That Changed Me

Travel didn't just show me new places-it revealed new pieces of myself. Every country, every culture, every quiet moment in a place I didn't know changed me in ways I didn't expect but deeply needed.

1. **Leaving home helps you see it more clearly.**

Sometimes, you can't truly appreciate what shaped you until you're far enough away to really look at it.

2. **You grow when you're uncomfortable.**

Not knowing the language, the customs, or the rules taught me to listen more, judge less, and trust my instincts.

3. **Humility is the passport to connection.**

When you enter someone else's world with respect, doors open that no guidebook can promise.

4. **Stillness exists in unexpected places.**

Whether on a train in Japan or a river in the Amazon, I found peace I didn't know I was looking for.

5. **Laughter is universal.**

You don't need to speak the same language to connect. A shared smile, a moment of joy-that's enough.

6. **You don't just collect stamps-you collect perspective.**

Each destination gave me a new lens to see myself and others. It expanded my world from the inside out.

7. **The most powerful discoveries are internal.**

I thought I was just visiting new places. But really, I was being reintroduced to myself-over and over again.

Lessons Learned — Chapter 7: When the World Changed Overnight

COVID-19 didn't just shut down the world-it exposed it.

It revealed the noise we relied on, the routines we hid behind, and the truths we didn't want to face.

For me, it stripped everything back until all I had left was myself-and the silence.

1. **Crisis doesn't build character-it reveals it.**

When everything stopped, I discovered who I really was without the job, the noise, or the distractions. It was humbling-but necessary.

2. **The world can change overnight-and so can you.**

Nothing is promised. Not time. Not routine. Not even breath. That realization changed how I show up every day now.

3. **The absence of noise doesn't mean peace.**

At first, the quiet felt like relief. But eventually, it became a mirror I couldn't look away from. That silence forced me to confront myself.

4. **Grief comes in waves-and many forms.**

It wasn't just the loss of people. It was the loss of normal, safety, and certainty. That grief is valid, even if no one names it.

5. **You don't realize how distracted you've been until stillness hits.**

The lockdown made space for reflection-but it also forced me to sit with things I'd avoided for years.

6. **Healing begins in the hard pause.**

That pause, as painful as it was, gave me time to begin-to heal, forgive, remember, and reclaim.

7. **The storm stripped away what didn't matter-and spotlighted what did.**

At the end of the day, it wasn't money, status, or schedules that mattered. It was people. Purpose. Peace. Breath.

Lessons Learned — Chapter 8: The War Within

The hardest battles I ever fought didn't involve bullets-they involved memories. Fears. Flashbacks. In silence, I faced an enemy that didn't wear a uniform but lived inside me.

1. **Just because you can't see the wound doesn't mean it's not real.**

Mental battles are invisible-but they're no less violent. The bruises may not show, but the pain runs deep.

2. **Denial delays healing.**

I told myself I was fine for years. But silence didn't save me-it suffocated me. Healing didn't begin until I spoke the truth out loud.

3. **Trauma doesn't leave on its own.**

It lingers. It disguises itself as anger, silence, or control. You have to name it to fight it.

4. **You are allowed to ask for help.**

That was the hardest lesson of all. I was raised to handle it, hide it, and harden up. But strength also means knowing when to reach out.

5. **Your mind can become a battlefield if you don't maintain it.**

This is My New Foundation

Without care, it becomes a loop of fear, shame, and worst-case scenarios. Peace isn't passive-it's something you have to protect.

6. **Feeling broken is not the same as being defeated.**

Some days, I felt like I was drowning in my own thoughts. But surviving those days made me stronger than I ever knew.

7. **You are not what happened to you-you are what you have healed from.**

I thought my story ended in pain. But that was just the turning point. I am not my trauma. I am my recovery.

This is My New Foundation

Lessons Learned — Chapter 9: Building in the Aftermath

I could decide what to do next. That's when resilience stopped being a buzzword-and became a blueprint.

1. **Resilience isn't what you show others-it's what you practice in private.**

It's waking up when you don't want to. Speaking truth when it's uncomfortable. Holding on when giving up would be easier.

2. **You can't rebuild with the same tools that broke you.**

I had to let go of old ways-pride, isolation, control-and pick up new ones: vulnerability, reflection, grace.

3. **Moving forward doesn't mean forgetting.**

I carried the pain with me-but I stopped letting it led me. Healing isn't erasing the past. It's reimagining your future.

4. **Small steps count.**

One prayer. One phone call. One good day after a week of bad ones. It all adds up. Progress doesn't have to be loud.

5. **Purpose grows in cracked soil.**

This is My New Foundation

I found meaning in the mess. Pain gave me vision. Loss gave me clarity. What nearly destroyed me defined me.

6. **You don't need a map-just the courage to take the next step.**

I didn't have all the answers. But I had enough strength to try again. That was enough to change everything.

7. **A future built from truth is stronger than one built on fear.**

I used to build walls. Now I build bridges-with my words, my faith, and my presence. That's resilience redefined.

Lessons Learned — Chapter 10: The Blessing in the Storm

I didn't ask for the storm. I didn't pray for the silence, the isolation, the pain. But in the middle of it all, something sacred happened. I met myself again. And I met God again-on new terms.

1. **Storms don't just strip-they reveal.**

When the distractions blew away, I saw clearly what mattered, who mattered, and what had to change.

2. **Crisis can be the doorway to calling.**

The world falling apart forced me to stop running. And in that stillness, I found my voice-and my purpose.

3. **Sometimes God answers prayers by clearing the room.**

I lost people. I lost comfort. But I also lost the noise. And in that emptiness, God made room for truth.

4. **Every breakdown carries a breakthrough-if you're willing to stay in it.**

I was shattered. But the pieces didn't stay on the floor. I started rebuilding slowly-and realized I was becoming something stronger.

5. **The blessing isn't always obvious.**

Sometimes the blessing is the storm. Because without it, I would've kept pretending, performing, surviving. The storm woke me up.

6. **Service is healing.**

When I started reaching out-sharing, helping, and writing–I stopped bleeding. My healing deepened when I poured into others.

7. **Peace isn't the absence of struggle. It's the presence of truth.**

The storm didn't take away my problems-but it forced me to stop lying to myself. That honesty became peace.

Lessons Learned — Chapter 11: Laying a New Foundation

Everything I had known-the trauma, the identity, the soldier's instinct, the broken silence-brought me to this moment. And this time, I wasn't standing on fear, pride, or performance. I was standing on truth.

1. **You can't build something new on a broken blueprint.**

I had to stop repeating patterns that no longer served me. Pain taught me how to survive. But now, I had to learn how to live.

2. **Foundations aren't flashy-they're forged in quiet decisions.**

It wasn't a single breakthrough. It was showing up every day-being real, being present, being willing to start again.

3. **Self-worth has to be rebuilt, not remembered.**

I didn't just wake up one day feeling whole. I had to dig through the wreckage of who I'd been to find who I could become.

4. **Healing takes architecture.**

It's not just a feeling-it's a process. A design. A decision to stop patching over damage and start laying something solid.

5. **You must build with truth-or it will collapse under pressure.**

I couldn't lie to myself anymore. Every time I did, the foundation cracked. Honesty became the cornerstone.

6. **Who you become matters more than what you survived.**

I used to wear survival like a badge. Now, I wear growth. Strength doesn't mean pain-it means progress.

7. **The new you deserve a strong place to stand.**

I'm not who I was before the storm. And I don't want to be. That old life served its purpose. This new one is mine-designed with intention, faith, and peace.

Lessons Learned — Chapter 12: A Life Shaped by Truth

Truth doesn't always arrive gently. Sometimes it disrupts. Sometimes it destroys. But when the dust settles, it's the only thing strong enough to build a life on.

1. **Truth is not just spoken-it's lived.**

It's not about what you say-it's about how you show up, how you treat people, how you carry your past, and how you face your future.

2. **You cannot heal from what you continue to hide.**

The pain I avoided became poison. But when I faced it-truly faced it-healing finally began.

3. **Living in truth doesn't mean life gets easier.**

It means you stop lying to yourself to make others comfortable. And that's where real freedom begins.

4. **You cannot be fully loved until you're fully known.**

I spent years wearing armor, smiling through silence. But true connection came when I let people see the real me-scars and all.

5. **There is no peace in pretending.**

Pretending wears, you out. It's a slow death. I found peace the moment I stopped performing and started being.

6. **Owning your truth helps others find theirs.**

Telling my story gave others permission to tell theirs. My honesty created a ripple I never saw coming.

7. **Truth is a daily choice, not a one-time confession.**

Every day, I decide to walk in it, speak it, and lead with it. That's how a life shaped by truth is built-moment by moment.

Lessons Learned — Chapter 13: There's One More Truth

For so long, I stayed silent in rooms where I should've spoken. Invisible in moments I should've been seen. But here's the truth I had to learn late in life: just because they didn't notice doesn't mean I didn't matter.

1. **You are not invisible-you are unseen.**

There's a difference. People may miss you, but that doesn't erase your impact. You are real. You are valuable. You leave a mark.

2. **Silence can be strength-but it can also be a prison.**

I wore silence like armor. But after a while, it stopped protecting me and started isolating me.

3. **Your story matters, even if it makes others uncomfortable.**

Some truths are hard to tell. But they need to be told-not for them, but for you.

4. **Recognition is not the same as worth.**

I had to separate my value from other people's acknowledgment. I mattered long before anyone clapped for me.

5. **Shame thrives in secrecy-truth sets you free.**

I used to think certain parts of my story had to stay buried. But naming them gave me power, healing, clarity.

6. **You don't have to yell to be heard.**

Sometimes, the most powerful messages come in whispers-in presence, in authenticity. Truth doesn't have to be loud-it just has to be real.

7. **Your existence is a testimony.**

Every day you wake up, breathe, and show up-you prove that your life has meaning. Whether the world sees it or not.

Lessons Learned — Chapter 14: What Tried to Break Me, Built Me

Pain was my first teacher. It didn't ask permission. It didn't wait until I was ready. It just came-loud, sudden, and unforgettable. But now I see what it came to do. It didn't come to break me. It came to build me.

1. **Pain isn't punishment-it's process.**

It doesn't mean you did something wrong. Sometimes, pain is the refining fire that pulls the truth to the surface.

2. **Growth begins where comfort ends.**

I never changed when things were easy. Real transformation started the moment it hurt too much to stay the same.

3. **You can either carry pain or be carried by it.**

For years, I let pain define me. Now, I define what it means. I use it. I speak from it. I don't hide it.

4. **What scars you also strengthens you.**

My wounds became wisdom. The same moments that nearly destroyed me now make me unshakable.

5. **Pain teaches what peace cannot.**

Peace soothes, but pain sharpens. Pain made me aware-of who I am, what I want, and what I will never allow again.

6. **There's purpose in the breaking.**

Not everything I lost was meant to stay. Sometimes, pain cleared the way for what I actually needed.

7. **I was not undone by the fire-I was refined by it.**

Pain burned away the lies. The pride. The silence. And what remained? Something solid. Something worthy. Something real.

Lessons Learned — Chapter 15: Strengthened by Love The Quiet Force That Kept Me Standing

Through every storm, every loss, and every silent battle… love stayed. It didn't always speak loudly, but it never left. Love became my anchor, my mirror, my medicine. And in the end, it became my greatest strength.

1. **Love is not weakness-it's reinforcement.**

I used to believe love made you soft. But real love? The kind that holds you in your darkest hour? That's where strength is born.

2. **Love doesn't always show up in words.**

It's in the steady hand. The quiet presence. The meals cooked. The eyes that say, "I see you," when the world looks past you.

3. **Love has the power to rewrite identity.**

For years, I believed I wasn't worthy. But the people who stayed, who saw me, loved me anyway-they showed me another version of myself. A truer one.

4. **Love is healing in motion.**

Each act of grace, each moment of understanding, each undeserved kindness-they stitched the broken parts of me back together.

5. **You don't have to earn love.**

That was a hard one. I thought I had to perform. Provide. Protect. But love that's real doesn't require perfection-just presence.

6. **Love reveals what trauma tries to bury.**

The child inside me who longed to feel safe? He found safety in the arms of real love. And that safety gave me back my voice.

7. **Love is legacy.**

What we give in love doesn't die with us. It echoes through our children, our friendships, our stories. This chapter, this life-I wrote it with love.

Faith didn't come to me in lightning bolts or miracles. It came in whispers, in stillness, in survival. It came when everything else fell apart, and I was still standing. Faith wasn't the absence of fear-it was the decision to walk through it.

8. **Faith doesn't have to be loud to be real.**

I used to think strong faith meant shouting, praising, and pushing through. But sometimes, the strongest faith is quiet-"Lord, help me breathe today."

9. **Belief doesn't always feel like certainty.**

There were days I doubted. Days I questioned. But faith isn't about having all the answers-it's about trusting while you search for them.

10. **Faith grows in dark places.**

When I couldn't see the way forward, faith reminded me that light still existed. I just had to keep moving.

11. **Trusting God doesn't mean you won't feel pain.**

I felt it all-loss, betrayal, grief. But faith carried me through it. Not around it-through it.

12. **Surrender is strength.**

Letting go didn't make me weak. It made space-for healing, for grace, for something bigger than me.

13. **Prayer is a lifeline, not a last resort.**

I stopped praying only when I was desperate. I started praying because I needed direction, not just rescue.

14. **God never left-I just stopped looking.**

Even in my silence, even in my anger, even in my numbness-He stayed. Waiting. Patient. Present.

Lessons Learned — Chapter 16: Reclaiming Life During COVID-19 on the River

The river didn't ask me to perform. It didn't need me to explain who I was. It just flowed-steady, clear, real. And somehow, in that stillness, I found the version of myself I thought was lost.

1. **Nature doesn't heal you-it reminds you.**

The trees, the water, the sky-they reminded me that peace isn't something you chase. It's something you allow.

2. **Stillness is a survival skill.**

I spent my life in motion, running from memory, grief, and silence. But on that river, stillness became my strength.

3. **The world may have shut down-but my spirit woke up.**

In a time of loss and lockdown, I found something sacred: my breath. My center. My ability to just be.

4. **God speaks in quiet places.**

The river became my sanctuary-not with stained glass or sermons-but with rhythm, air, and space to listen.

5. **You can reclaim your life without shouting.**

I didn't need to announce my healing. I just needed to live it-day by day, step by step, breath by breath.

6. **You don't have to be productive to be valuable.**

The river taught me that rest is holy. That worth isn't measured by work-but by presence.

7. **Sometimes healing wears waders and waits in the water.**

Out there, I wasn't a title, a veteran, or a survivor. I was just a man-breathing, healing, remembering who he was.

Lessons Learned — Chapter 17: Marion "Money" Browder – The Brother Who Taught Me Grace

He was steady when I was shaken. Quiet when I was loud. Protective when I didn't know I needed protecting. "Money" wasn't just my brother-he was a part of my foundation.

1. **Brotherhood is a bond, not a title.**

We didn't always say it, but we knew it. Blood made us family-but loyalty made us brothers.

2. **The best protectors don't need permission.**

Money didn't ask questions-he handled business. His love showed up without fanfare, but it showed up every time.

3. **Real love shows up in the shadows.**

He didn't want the spotlight. He was the spotlight for those who needed someone to believe in them, defend them, or just be there.

4. **Your story is shaped by who stands beside you.**

I wouldn't be who I am without him. His presence helped me survive things I didn't know were survivable.

5. **Quiet strength is still strength.**

Money didn't yell to be heard. He didn't push to be praised. But his impact echoes louder than most people's speeches.

6. **Some angels wear hoodies, not halos.**

He wasn't perfect, but he was real. Sometimes, that's exactly what you need to feel safe in a world that tries to break you.

7. **Brotherhood leaves a legacy.**

Even when he's not in the room, his lessons, his love, and his example walk with me. That's forever.

Lessons Learned — Chapter 18: A Son Who Loved His Mom with Respect—By Any Means

She was my first home. My first protector. The first person to show me what unconditional love looked like-and the last person whose approval I ever needed.

1. **A mother's love is the blueprint for your worth.**

She taught me how to carry myself, to be strong, to be respectful, and to never forget where I came from.

Love doesn't have to be perfect to be powerful.

She didn't always have the answers, but she had enough love to cover every flaw. That love shaped me.

2. **A mother's presence never leaves you.**

Even when she was gone, her voice stayed-in the way I treat people, in the way I walk, in the way I pray.

3. **Protecting your mother is a sacred duty.**

I carried that responsibility with pride. No title I've ever held means more to me than being her son.

4. **Grief is love with nowhere to go.**

Losing her didn't end our relationship-it changed it. Now I love her in silence, in legacy, in remembrance.

5. **A mother's wisdom lives in the quiet things.**

The things she used to say, the meals she made, the glances that told me everything-they're still with me.

6. **Love doesn't die. It transforms.**

What we shared lives in every story I tell, every lesson I pass on, every time I say, "She made me who I am."

Lessons Learned — Chapter 19: This Is My New Foundation

I spent years trying to survive on cracked ground. Running on empty. Living on pride. Fighting ghosts. But the storm taught me what the silence confirmed-I needed something new. Something real. Something mine. This is what I built. Not from comfort, but from clarity. Not from fear, but from faith.

1. **You don't have to rebuild what broke you.**

The old life wasn't sustainable. It got me here, but it can't take me forward. That's why I started fresh-on truth.

2. **Foundations are not built in public.**

The strongest parts of me were built in private. In pain. In prayer. In the dark. Where nobody could see-but where everything changed.

3. **Peace is a decision, not a destination.**

I stopped waiting to feel better and started building better. That choice became peace.

4. **You can't borrow identity-you have to claim it.**

I let go of who others said I had to be. Now I stand as who I am-fully, unapologetically, and freely.

5. **What you walk away from can be just as holy as what you walk into.**

This is My New Foundation

I left behind survival mode. Silence. Shame. That release was sacred.

6. **A solid foundation starts with forgiveness.**

Of others. Of life. Of myself. Only then could I begin to build something that would last.

7. **Your new beginning can start whenever you decide.**

There's no magic day. No perfect moment. I just chose to begin. And that choice changed everything.

Author Bio

Bill Bailey is a retired U.S. Army Warrant Officer, entrepreneur, and founder of Rapier Solutions, a thriving Service-Disabled Veteran-Owned Small Business. A Detroit native, Bill's life has been defined by discipline, resilience, and an unwavering faith that has carried him through 26 years of military service—13 active and 13 reserve. In his military career, he earned recognition for his leadership in high-pressure environments and his ability to innovate within the realm of enterprise IT.

However, beneath these impressive titles and achievements lies a much deeper story. Bill's early life was marked by childhood trauma, adversity, and premature responsibility. It was through the structure of the military and the purpose found in entrepreneurship that he began to heal and find direction. His personal journey, however, took a pivotal turn when COVID-19 forced a pause, allowing him to confront the silent pain that had shaped much of his life.

In his memoir, *This Is My New Foundation*, Bill Bailey shares his story not to glorify the past, but to empower others who are facing their own battles. He speaks with raw honesty about his experiences—childhood trauma, a spiritual awakening, and the ongoing process of mental health reckoning. His work is rooted in truth, strengthened by love, and guided by unshakable faith.

Through this memoir, Bill offers a roadmap for those who have carried silent pain, providing hope, healing, and a path to renewal. His life, both personal and professional, is a testament to the power of resilience, faith, and the determination to rise above the challenges that define us.

Bill now lives in North Carolina with his wife, Hazel, where he continues to mentor veterans, support his community, and build a legacy anchored in the principles of service, strength, and restoration. *This Is My New Foundation* is a powerful reminder that no matter the struggles we face, there is always an opportunity for transformation and renewal.

www.ingramcontent.com/pod-product-compliance
Lightning Source LLC
Chambersburg PA
CBHW070054080526
44586CB00013B/1045